From DOOMED to DOCTOR
280 Chestnut Street

Dear Marie,

Thank so much for your support!

Love + hugs

Dr. Senior

From DOOMED to DOCTOR
280 Chestnut Street

BORN IN THE CRACK BUT
DIDN'T FALL THROUGH

―⚬⚬⚬―

Dr. Bonita J. Gay-Senior

© 2017 Dr. Bonita J. Gay-Senior
All rights reserved.

ISBN-13: 9781541250130
ISBN-10: 1541250133
Library of Congress Control Number: 2016921331
CreateSpace Independent Publishing Platform
North Charleston, South Carolina

Dedication

This book is dedicated to my two brothers, Danny Lamar Gay and Kenneth Lee Gay, who perished right before my eyes from the effects of childhood abuse, and the silent mental illness of schizophrenia. Also to my sister Debbie Yvonne Gay whose whereabouts have been unknown to the family for many years for the same reasons.

Table of Contents

Preface · ix

Part One: Early Life · 1
Part Two: Pre-Teen to College Life · · · · · · · · · · · · 41
Part Three: Looking For Healthy Love · · · · · · · · · · · 63
Part Four: Personal Growth · · · · · · · · · · · · · · · · · · 93

Epilogue · 157
Acknowledgements · · · · · · · · · · · · · · · · · · · 161

Preface

THIS BOOK IS A TRUE story about my life that took a long time to write because it includes many dark times that I would rather not remember. Nonetheless, I felt my life story could give others the courage to conquer their life obstacles, no matter how it began. I was able to create a new life regardless of how bad things once were. It takes time to change, to regain and reclaim all that was lost as a result of childhood abuse, neglect and bullying.

It centered on my family of origin: four brothers, one sister, my mom and grandmother. Their names in chronological order from the oldest to the youngest: Danny, Kenneth, Billie Rank, Randy and Debbie and there is Mom Beulah and Grandma Mary. From birth to 18 things at home were brutal – my mother and five siblings were plagued with painful human flaws. I never knew what to expect on a daily basis. It was as if we were all trapped in the family tragedy. Through no choice of my own, I was subjected to daily suffering.

To escape it all I turned to movies, music and TV programs. Thus, in my story I will reference them often. They are considered "classics" now and R&B Old School music. Yet the themes are ageless. The themes of home, faith, love, success, romance, validation, confirmation, friendship and life experiences never go out of style – they are simply expressed differently.

Each song, movie or TV series gave me a source of comfort and encouragement. Many times these things were an unfailing source of love and affection in a seemingly hopeless situation. To be exact they became my animated imaginary friends as I was too ashamed to tell anyone about my living circumstances for fear I would be blamed. The well-known documented fact of a child's mind that says, "It's gotta be my fault!!!"

I was 48 when I received my Doctorate of Education degree from Clark Atlanta University in Atlanta, Georgia. As I stood in line waiting for these established distinguished professors to call my name to receive my degree, indescribable joy and gratitude flooded my being. Upon hearing my name, I walked across the stage feeling God's love hugging me! A sweet feeling came over me and instructed me to now go out and tell the world that you can "Repair Your Life!"

The one thing that got my attention from age 18 to 26 was that I was repeating the same painful experiences even though I was no longer helpless at the mercy of mom Beulah and my five siblings. That is when I decided to work hard at life as well as study it. A poignant saying sums it up succinctly: "I can do nothing to change the past except stop repeating it in the present!"

I took tiny actions each day that proved to me to be more effective than weeks and months of immobility followed by forceful attempts to change quickly. My process was simple not easy: own up, admit my faults, make up, forgive myself and others continually, keep up, continue to learn about myself, religion, God(The Source Of Creation) and help others.

Spirituality was the rock upon which I built my second life presented in this book. I hope it empowers you as it did me!

Part One: Early Life

"We are born into human laboratories called 'families.' What happened to us is our beginning, under the roof we call home, will affect us for the rest of our lives. No matter how far we travel, how fast we run, we carry home with us wherever we go. Many times we leave home carrying heavy suitcases packed with misconceptions, anger and with feelings we should have expressed."

PATRICE GAINS, "MOMENTS OF GRACE"

Early Life

I was a dead woman walking at the age of 27. My life had been one piercing disaster after another. My day to day living was churning, swirling out of control, a real "hot mess," and I was clueless as to why. It felt somewhat like a 9/11 morning catastrophe, one horror after another: except my attackers were from my own insides and I was powerless to stop the daily fires that left me scarred with emotional and mental blisters. It felt like I was riding on a merciless merry-go-round, at the whim of Hurricane Katrina winds, and drowning in a sea of self-made flood waters. I began to see them as emotional disasters.

Luckily, being naturally somewhat intelligent, I began a quest to connect the dots. It was crystal clear at this point that I was doomed to hell on earth if I didn't do something drastic, so I chose the road less traveled for many years: the road of facing myself and all of my demons, owning my part of this haunting nightmare, and setting out to reconstruct my life. It turned out to be a tremendous endeavor. I needed a new Bonita, one who could make constructive decisions instead of destructive ones. Life is merely a series of choices and reactions. Good ones, which can heal us; bad ones, which can hurt us; or indifferent ones which won't have much of an effect.

My journey is too horrific for most people to comprehend, and it began on St. Patrick's Day, March 17, 1956. It is ironic that I was born on a day considered to be lucky. Yes, sometimes it did feel like God was teasing me, because luck was exactly what it took to drive my humble beginnings toward a new, uncharted path. I like to think of it as God luck…the miraculous! I would need luck…light- years of it to overcome the pathology of the generational dysfunction in my family.

Hot Stuff: In the Name of Family

My early years were filled with chaos; I endured a bitter loneliness. I recall waking up one morning to a burning house, full of smoke. I was shaken awake by my oldest brother, to a blazing hot feeling, and I began to cry uncontrollably. In my young mind, I was thinking, "Why? How? Who? What? When? Who would want to burn our house down, and with all seven of us in it?"

It happened in the dead of night; all seven of us scrambled to get outside. Smoke and heat were everywhere, but we managed to make it out safely. We had escaped what turned out to be a premeditated murder attempt. I was four years old, and I have some memories of the event. My mom and brother retold the story on several occasions as did aunts, uncles, and first cousins. Here is an account of the events.

Our last stay in the Eagan Home Projects ended with an eviction, and our rent-a-house cycle went full-blown. In between evictions, babies kept coming, and long stays at Grandma's house began. This went on for 10 agonizing years. On many occasions, our dad left us without food and homeless, and finally, my mother, Beulah, had enough. She separated from my dad even though this was unheard of in the 1960s and frowned upon by her mother, Mary, Grandma Mary to me!

My mom had finally left dad for good, and he was furious. Our father, Willie Frank Gay Sr., was known to not work, get drunk, and gamble, Dad was too self-absorbed to realize he couldn't keep his wife and his six children that way. It finally set in when he realized mom Beulah was serious about leaving him. So he decided the best solution was to wait until we were all at home, tucked into our beds, fast asleep, then he poured gasoline on the house, hoping to kill all seven of us. Of course, he had to get really stupid drunk to do this, and that's exactly what he did. We were swiftly taken to Grandma Mary's house.

Mom Beulah had finally stood up to him. She went to the police station and took out a warrant. Mom Beulah told them who did it, and why he did it. Dad was arrested, but later released because she didn't have any witnesses. However, there was a traveling rumor throughout Dad's side of the family that he'd said, "Yes, I tried to burn those suckers up!"

This time, our stay at Grandma Mary's house was short lived because Grandmother and Mom didn't get along. They had an atrocious relationship. The shouting matches between them frightened me, my brothers and my sister. A soothing day finally came, Mom Beulah found a house for us. I inhaled and exhaled with excitement as we moved to our new home. Glory, glory—the evictions came to a permanent halt, and the moving from house to house faded into the sunset as quickly as it came. At last it was 284 Chestnut Street!

Then, a new form of insanity settled among my living arrangements: all of a sudden, I was tossed in the salad with six family members: Danny, Kenneth, Randy, Billie Rank, mother Beulah, and my sister, Princess to Queen Debbie. Early on, I always felt like an outsider—a misfit.

My dad had always kept my brothers in line. With his presence, they didn't dare harass me but he was gone. Mom Beulah was absent a lot too as she worked and went to school to become a hairstylist; eventually, owning her own hair salon.

At first, I was so happy to be at 284 Chestnut Street in this two-room house with one kitchen, and one front room, as we called it in those days. According to my oldest brother, we had lived in many places before settling down on Chestnut Street. These places were always in "the hood," low-income neighborhoods, except that in the 1950s and 1960s it wasn't called "the hood." It seemed as if many African Americans lived in broken down shacks or one of the housing projects. We had our share of both. The Eagan Home Government Projects was luxury living in the eyes of my oldest brother, Danny. I was too young to remember or to know the difference. It was only decades later, he realized that living in the projects was actually a poverty-stricken state of living and not the penthouse suite his childhood mind once envisioned.

We liked our new house! The males had a room in the kitchen and the females had the other room, and better than that, one day out of the blue, mother Beulah brought home a television set.

I had a close relationship with that television set. It was my only means of escape, except for the large quantities of food. I was so mesmerized by the morals in the shows and I especially liked the romance scenes when the boy finally kisses the girl. Suddenly, I knew how I wanted my life to be. It would be like the TV shows, with a happy ending—*It's a Wonderful Life*, Jimmy Stewart type of life! "Teacher says, Every time a bell rings, an angel gets his wings."

Whoops, unexpected blow. I am being screamed at by mom Beulah. "I'm going to leave all six of you kids. I'm sick of you all!" Kazzaam: Mom is making those cutting remarks again. "Get your damn ass in here and sweep this kitchen." Thoughts race through my head. What? What? Where the hell am I? This certainly doesn't match the TV shows, *Dick Van Dyke,* or *Captain Kangaroo*. It's a million-man march away from the *Popeye Club* and the *Lone Ranger*. No one acted like this on the *Lassie* show. I embraced TV, and it was my world. It gave me a path to disconnect from the madness of my first family.

I felt like things were going pretty doggone well (the TV, no drunk Dad), until we moved three houses over to 280 Chestnut Street. This new house had three rooms instead of two. Almost immediately, I developed anxiety from the move and had a miserable time adjusting. I couldn't give it a name at the time, but today, it is clear to me. You see, my only means of comfort had vanished. The one television that we had was now moved to my brothers' room. Never again did I have access to the TV. All my favorite shows faded into a memory—like a vapor—and so did I, heartbroken.

My brothers took it away from me like prisoners are taken away and locked in a cell. I knew where the TV was but they prevented me from getting to it. The TV we had was being controlled by my abusers. The one thing that kept me company was gone. I held all these feelings inside, as I had long since stopped talking to mother Beulah. All she did was scream, yell, fuss, and beat your ass with an electrical extension cord over the slightest flaw. I was fragile, and Grandma Mary wasn't much help because she had little to no influence over her daughter, mother Beulah. Left with no one to tell, I descended into a bottomless pit of the damned, which was a breeding ground for assorted addictions. I ate just about everything I could find—and it began to show on my young body.

With my TV crutch gone, the horror of it all seemed too commonplace at 280 Chestnut Street. My house was the last of three houses in an alley. In those days, there were still unpaved sidewalks in Atlanta. It felt like a dark cave. However, the welfare food of yellow grits, canned spam, canned beef, powdered eggs, dry beans, white rice, powdered milk, white flour, and yellow cornmeal was an welcoming sight. In addition, hors d'oeuvres to us was store-bought white bread, hot dogs, red hot links, pork and beans, and sweet Kool-Aid. It made me smile when we finally had something different to eat.

Many days our meal was a pot of beans and a pan of cornbread. Another entrée was cornbread and buttermilk. Again, I'd smile for this dish, as did my five siblings but I ate large quantities of these foods---any foods! Strangely, Mom would never eat with us. She had her meals elsewhere, and then she retired to her locked (no children allowed) room. Well, except for my youngest sister, Queen Debbie. Debbie could stay in Mom's room 24/7, without any harsh words or harmful side effects. She and Mom had an emotionally unhealthy relationship, which possibly could have influenced her in her later years to date both men and women. I ain't mad at yah! Do *YOU!!!*

Getting Lost

In between attending school and eating whatever I could find, I would lay on my roll-away bed and think. I recalled the time when I was five and got lost trying to impress mom Beulah.

One day she asked me to go to the store to buy my baby sister some carnation milk for her bottle, "Oh, boy," I thought. "This is my chance to get her to like me." I recall being ecstatic when she selected *me,* and not my brothers, to go to the neighborhood store in Vine City, Atlanta, at the corner of Chestnut Street and Simpson Road.

I was going to make her proud. Sheer joy ran through my body. Wow, she finally noticed me, and actual words rolled out of her mouth, as she said, "Bonita, I want you to go to the store, and get a can of Pet Carnation Milk for your baby sister's bottle." I said OKAY to my mom Beulah with pride.

I happily and joyously strutted my five-year-old self down to the nearby store, owned by Jewish Americans. Surely I could get my mother to like me now. I'd be her errand runner to the store when she ran out of things.

Well, I made it to the store and got the milk. Boy, oh boy, I felt like a World Series recipient. What I didn't know back then, but I know now, is that I am geographically challenged—as in no natural sense of direction. At age five, I walked out of the store, and there were four possible directions to go. I stood there in a panic, my confidence plummeted, and I felt sheer terror. I thought to myself, "Do I go left, or do I go right?"

Everything seemed so gigantic, the store, the houses, the streets, the cars, even the intersection appeared to be huge, and I began to shrink. All I could think about was not being able to please mother Beulah. I could almost see, taste, and feel her stench of disappointment. The last thing on my mind was to be imperfect to mother Beulah again. I then made a choice to turn left. As I look back, I was halfway correct. All I needed to do was just add another quick left to my directions.

I began my tombstone walk for home. Each time I saw a familiar house or street, my delight would soar, only to take a jabbing dive as I realized I was mistaken again. I walked and cried, cried and walked! I walked some more, and I cried some more, knowing that I had failed to make mother

Beulah happy. Exhausted and defeated, I went to a house and knocked on a door and a lovely, caring lady answered. I said to the well-kept lady, "I am lost." She invited me in and gave me a glass of cold milk—real cow milk (the best I had ever tasted). It was so different from the welfare, dry, nonfat milk in my house. In addition, she gave me a wonderful tasting slice of coconut cake.

It felt so good to be in a two-parent house. The house was orderly and clean and there was lots of food. More noticeable than all of those things was the atmosphere of the house; it blew me away. It was so sweet and loving.

This gentle home situation resonated through my body, and I made a snapshot of it in my mind. I set a subconscious goal for myself that day, at the age of five, that I would have a family like this one day. Somehow I knew that I'd like to aspire to a functional home life like that for myself and my family. I experienced the presence of goodness that day, and unknowingly, it positively impacted my way of thinking and living forever.

This family home was so different from the one I knew. Mine was filled with discord on a minute-by-minute basis. I don't remember the nice lady's name. She called the police and reported me as a lost child. Mom Beulah had also called the police to report that I was missing. Within a few minutes, a policeman arrived and drove me home. I never saw that *Cinderella, Huxtable, Leave It to Beaver* family again, but I was determined to have some portion of what they had. One day I would overcome my skin peeling, drama filled beginning. I held tightly to my goal, my dream and my destiny.

I arrived home and jumped out of the officer's car. For the first time in my life, mother Beulah hugged me and was happy to see me! While in her embrace, my insides lit up. Later, when she retold the story, she always bragged to others that I still had the can of milk and the exact change in my hand, even though I had gotten lost. I'd wanted to do *something* right, so I held on to the money and the milk—two out of three ain't bad! After a while, the episode faded into oblivion. It was back to the reality of living on Chestnut Street.

Pot Talking to the Kettle

Things got really weird once dad was permanently gone, mom Beulah turned into this mean, angry human. I did see compassion from her for Debbie. But as for me, it was no surprise that I was not my mother's favorite child. I conjured up all kinds of reasons to explain why she openly disliked me; maybe I didn't wash the dishes good enough or maybe I didn't smile enough, or the right way. I always felt her hatred for me was somehow my fault. Years later, it became acutely clear that my skin color played a huge part in being neglected by my mom. She favored my sister Debbie over me because she had "good hair" and was "light skinned" – a *Learned Prejudice* forced upon my ethnic group from mainstream America dating back to the 1700's. It still existed among some group within the then labeled "Negro" community during the 1960s. I, on the other hand, was born brown complexion (nutmeg), and this color was not widely accepted at that time due to misinformation that was directly derived from the Black Holocaust of innocent African Americans stolen from their motherland and forced to do free labor.

In fact, my brothers wouldn't say, "brown" as my skin color; instead they would say, "Black." I was actually considered to be crayon black, even though that was not my true skin color or my race because in the 1960s, African Americans were called, "Negroes" (derived from the Spanish language, meaning black. Today we are called African Americans or Blacks as our ethnic group). We knew our race and were quite proud of it but to be mean to one another, some would bully you in reference to the various shades of your skin pigmentation. Another example of this color saga is that whites are considered better off if they are tanned, the darker the better! Actually in fact, the true measure of a human being should be their daily character and not the amount of melanin or lack of it in their derma. There is too much wasted energy on colorism.

On a daily basis, I would hear the infamous Mom Beulah, unlocking her door padlocked door so sister Queen Debbie could enter what seemed to me Mom's palace in our one-bedroom home. I'd be left without a sister in the kitchen-turned-bedroom, with no entertainment and, no siblings to pass time with. It was enough to drive a kid *mad*. Instead, an invisible part of me cracked. Even some of my brothers favored my sister Debbie over me because I had short, soft, kinky hair –tightly curled, as Maya Angelou so sweetly rephrases. Really, I am of African descent. It was as if the human race had one acceptable image for a girl, and that was the Barbie doll look. One image does not fit all! Jeepers!

I have only one sister, and truth be told, I developed a strong dislike for her. She was my mom's last child – "baby girl," as society calls it! Hell, I didn't give a damn about any of that....Why was she treated like a real person, a human being, and I like an orphaned step-child? That just clawed at me. Moreover, Debbie is five years younger than me, and that age gap didn't help matters. She got the prettiest clothes, the fresh and hot-iron pressed hair with ribbons and quality time with mom Beulah. I, however, was on the sidelines, salivating for a fraction of what she was getting on a regular basis. A recipe for slow-simmering resentment soup was brewing. Resentments, layer by layer, over the years, grew into a mound of disgust. Fantasy thoughts floated in my subconscious: "I'll show...I'll show them all....You will all be sorry for treating me like black trash."

BEULAHVILLE

The neglect continued and there is nothing worse than emotional murder. No one can see the bleeding, the invisible parts of you being killed—the things done in the name of motherly love. Spending the first phase of my life with mom (until 18 years of age), was like being trapped in a revolving door—the chance of getting out was slim to none. She always overkilled the, "I am your mother" slogan. Those four words sent all six of us children spiraling downward into a rapid, bottomless hole of twisting, stabbing shame and guilt.

I can't tell you how many times I told myself, "But she's my mom. Mom's don't harm their children, so I must be overreacting." Consequently, I learned not to trust myself. I hated her, and my life. I couldn't make sense of it all—she was so mean; a ruthless tyrant who walked the line, leaning into being possessed by demonic forces. Hallelujah, she kept her abuse within the legal limits, and she never did illegal crimes, or persuaded us to do crimes. She believed in religion and sent us to church, and she would come some Sundays, as well.

Things were so out of balance in Beulahville. As mentioned, she openly favored my only sister over me and saw nothing wrong with her behavior. I wanted her affection really bad. Only twice I remember having her all to myself. We were at the Laundromat washing 12 loads of clothes or more. I followed her everywhere, like a puppy follows *his Master*. I couldn't take my eyes off of her. I was so glad to have one-to-one time with mom Beulah.

Then, out of the blue, she blasted me with these words: "Would you take your ass somewhere and sit down? Don't follow me anymore, dammit', you are getting on my nerves." I shrank right then and there, to a centimeter. I felt like my skin was ripped from my flesh. I felt like Nettie in *The Color Purple*. Why, why, why? She rarely left my sister, but as for me, I was a nuisance, an annoyance. From that moment on, I stayed as far away from her as I could. To my dismay, she liked it.

I was always comparing how I was treated to how my only sister Debbie was treated. We've all heard of the momma's boy. Well, mom Beulah took this to a whole different level with "momma's girl!" Reflecting back, I remember another event that tore the skin from my bones. I stood on the north side of our one-bedroom shack, drooling at the mouth like a dog does when he is begging for food. I stood there, at the north corner, frozen in my tracks as I saw my mother on the south side of the kitchen; happy, smiling, and hugging my sister. She brightened up in the presence of my sister. I ached for the same affection, touch, and approval, like the ones she gave Debbie. I felt like I would return to life, if she would just hug me once.

I was terrified of reaching out to her, because I could hear her voice, saying, "Will you take your ass somewhere and sit down? Don't follow me anymore." That incident in the Laundromat haunted me daily. So, instead of moving toward her for a sliver of affection, I just watched with the drooping eyes of the canine species.

Zap, once again, the inevitable happened. From out of nowhere, as if she was reading my mind, mom Beulah shouted at me with words that sliced me into tiny pieces. She said, "What are you staring at? I ain't never gonna hug you —you evil heifer," with a don't come near us posture. What the hell is a "heifer," I thought silently. At that moment, mom Beulah and my sister went into the locked living room. Mom Beulah had installed a deadbolt on her door to keep us out and away from her. I just stood there and sobbed my heart out, lost and turned out!

I was crushed like a grape — again. Years into the making, these crushed grapes would ferment and be turned into a fine wine. From that moment on, I permanently conditioned myself to never talk to my mother, and whenever she acknowledged my existence and spoke to me, I would respond with a pitiful, "Yes, Mother." My only form of retaliation was to pout and be passive-aggressive. If she entered the room, I tried to disappear by not looking at, or talking to her. I would just wait for the happy moment that she would leave the room, and lock her deadbolt.

It was a win for me if she left the room without placing a pounding slap to my face, as I did not talk to her even if she talked to me. I've always been fiery when pushed to the limit — but I must be pushed first. "Forget you," was my motto at this point. Now, I had spunk; once I reached my peak. By now, I had both hatred and fear of her at the same time.

Currently, and throughout my childhood, her overkill cop-out was, "All my children hate me!" Dang, do you not get it? If you're beating up your children with words, and beating them with electrical extension cords, they may not be responsive to that. Glory, I guess not!

I felt like an alien in that family environment. My natural spirit was to be kind, helpful and caring. I was full of good, but trapped in a house with evil. Either two out of my four brothers were tormenting me, or mom Beulah was punching me emotionally, or hitting me with unannounced slaps in the face, because I wouldn't talk to her – my only form of combat! She'd scream out, "You ain't never gonna keep no husband." I'm thinking, "Yo' ass ain't either."

In a sense, I can relate to Maya Angelou, who refused to talk for six years due to trauma. I refused to talk to mother Beulah after repeated heartaches! *Don't break my heart, my achy breaky heart* by Ray Cyrus describes it best. The slaps were less painful than her words.

Submerged in family abuse and neglect, I was deeply afraid to use the one bathroom we had at 280 Chestnut Street. I had to walk through our one bedroom, where all four of my brothers slept, watched TV, and lived. On a few occasions, two of my brothers crossed the line of what was considered appropriate gender behavior that left the residue of a shameful view of myself and an all-out sense of unworthiness. I felt like a misfit, a reject, and I would do anything to avoid using the bathroom. Once, when I was sitting on the toilet, my brother Kenneth pushed the bathroom door open. I was stunned and did not want him there, but I was unable to say, "Get the heck out of here!" So we talked, and then the unthinkable happened. My grandmother caught us. She was upset and irritated and began to lecture me as she often did about healthy sex actions. My grandmother would tell me repeatedly, to my disgust, that no boy, be it my brother, her brothers, or a stranger, is to touch me in a bad way. Also, she whipped me that day, and not my brother, which seemed damn unfair. Shit, he came in on me, not the other way around!

Her conversation was glued in my head and it really came in handy when another brother, Billie Rank, tried to molest me. From my earliest memory, he had a deep, sinister dislike for me. He called me derogatory names, day in and day out. I, on the other hand, really liked my big brother; our personalities and talents were similar. Both of us were quite smart, deep thinkers, as well as ambitious. Making good grades in school was effortless for us.

It is very tragic that it wasn't until my 40s that I realized my strengths and connected the dots as to why he didn't like me. It became super clear that it was for those very reasons that my brother Billie Rank hated me; because I was talented and could make good grades easily. This is why he would call me names, and tried to kill my spirit with incest. I was a threat to his ego. Yes, I was as gifted intellectually as he was. As a child, and for many years to come, I didn't see myself as bright. I would live as a wounded child from his verbal abuse and be clueless as to why he set out to destroy my personhood.

So as I said earlier, because my grandmother had educated me—perhaps it's better said that she *over*educated me about my brothers as well anyone else touching me in a yucky way—I was able to say, no to Billie Rank that sunny day, as he tried to convince me to lay down so he could play "doctor" with me. He offered all of his snacks and treats, but I could hear my grandmother scolding loud and clear at me. Her girl talk with me paid off big time, and I was able to be firm, with a rock solid "NO." Also, I recalled that I had gotten beaten when Kenneth, my other brother, had opened the bathroom door on me. Here I go again, the *Color Purple* call of "a girl-child ain't safe around a house full of boys." "All my life, I had to fight—but I'll kill him dead before I'm abused by any of em' in that way."

No dad, a mom who did not like me, two out of four brothers, and one sister who didn't like me, and at this point, I didn't like them either. What a living purgatory! Living in that three-room, one-bedroom shack, eating welfare food, and being abandoned and neglected by Mama. To make matters worse, I went from skinny to fat by age nine, was dark complexioned, with short nappy hair, and I was ugly, according to some of my family members. In addition, I felt enslaved by my grandmother to cook and clean her house obsessively. My saving grace was that she was nice to me. She always called me, "Sister." Looking back, I now know that my mom was hung up on her light-skinned complexion and felt she was superior for this reason. She thought less of dark-skinned women, such as me and her mother, my sweet granny. I guessed that she knew what was going on and saw its unfairness. She treated me good--- extra good!

Grandma Mary rallied for me and was my biggest supporter during those critical years. The older I get the more I cherish how she loved and nurtured me. I had mixed feelings about Grandma Mary. I liked how kind she was to me but despised the fact that she was grooming me to become a maid! She was a maid for much of her life for white people. The movie, *The Help,* meant a lot to me.

So, to add insult to injury, my mother Beulah sent me to my grandmother's house, against my wishes a lot! My grandmother lived four houses away, in the old 284 Chestnut Street house. I was left there for days and dared by my mother Beulah to return home. If I *did* sneak home, she would send me right back, while my sister stayed with her. I was the only sibling who was forced to spend days upon days with my grandmother. There were days when I thought death was better than this. Grandmother never stopped cooking and cleaning...I just wanted some play time.

My grandmother was a loving, warm and caring lady, but it was obvious that my mother didn't like her at all. I absorbed that, so I didn't like my grandmother as much as I should have either. In hindsight, my grandmother was a positive role model for me. I see her purpose in my life now. Years later, upon much reflection, I've come to love her dearly. Everything I know about religion, cooking, cleaning, values, and a work ethic, I learned from her. I salute Grandmother Mary's greatness.

The same is true with my oldest brother Danny I was so deeply deficient that only after experiencing years of life that I came to realize that he loved me as I was. He used to tell me all the time that our dad loved his baby girl (Bonita) and gave him the charge to watch out for me once he and my mom divorced.

Even though I became fat from the age of nine to 15, had short, cotton-like hair and was the color black (so they said), not once did Danny mistreat me! He was the one supportive person to me in the family…the family of pure evil, and evil it was. Once I became an adult, I recalled visiting my mother's beauty salon, and to my horror, she had hung a quotation plaque that said, "Live is 'evil', spelled backwards!"

My insides collapsed when I read it, and there was only one soft place to fall: my brother Danny. When I told him about the plaque, he shook his head, and said what he always said, "this family is cursed!" Years later, my sister Debbie (Mom's favorite), eventually ran away when mom Beulah threatened to shoot her over some disagreement, and the police was called. Sister Queen Debbie, Danny and I all came to the same conclusion: mother Beulah was wicked!

Speaking of validation, now three of her adult children, Danny, Debbie, and I could no longer deny the destructive nature of Mother Beulah. Continual damaging behavior and words shattered any hope of mistaken identity as the numbers increased from three to six who experienced the unthinkable words and threats of physical harm from mother Beulah. Even as adults we were not safe from the same violence. She threatened to shoot both Danny and Debbie on several occasions, and she threatened to attack me with a water hose, and she did all of this while attending several church services a week!

Billie Rank's Abuse: Meanest Brother Ever

My brother Billie Rank was two years older than me. He picked up on my mom's dislike for me, and the fact that I stayed as far away from her as I could made matters worse. I became his target. He would call me harsh names such as, "bald-headed, fat, ugly, and stinky" on a daily basis. This behavior went on for years, because I didn't want to tell my mother—I was afraid she would join in with him. He was her favorite son. I was too embarrassed to tell anyone. I fantasized that it would go away. It never did.

So to compensate, I ate large amounts of food; whatever I could find. My other brother, Kenneth, brother number two, and Billie Rank, brother number three, would team up on me with the name calling and bullying comments.

One of my most vivid memories of public humiliation occurred when I walked home from school through Eagan Home Public Housing. Several boys, including Kenneth and Billie Rank, were playing basketball. I was so scared when I saw them, because I knew they would start the name-calling and painful remarks. I tried to sneak past them quickly, but it didn't work.

To my dismay, it was worse than ever. Everybody on the basketball court stopped playing basketball and began making thoughtless, piercing remarks that rang in my brain for an eternity. "Look at your fat and ugly sister. Man, she is ugly, nappy hair, bald-headed...look at her clothes! Damn, what an ugly bitch! Is that your sister?" My brothers would reply, "No, she ain't. Yep, she is fat, ugly, with no hair. I don't know her." Name-calling and insults circled my world, and the verbal abuse attacks rose to a new level at home. My downfall was that I was silently taking it all in. I just kept on eating to deaden the pain. I never told a soul until I entered a healing group and got therapy years later as an adult.

We attended the same elementary school. The children in my neighborhood were rerouted from E. A. Ware Elementary School to E.R. Carter Elementary School because of our street address. Four siblings and I attended the school. We were all close to two years apart, which meant that four of us attended E. R. Carter at the same time, but in different grades. That was always comforting, even though we acted like we were unrelated when we were in school. My brothers were mean to me at school too! Gee, I didn't get a break!!

It was as if we were shell-shocked little people trapped in a zone of despair and sorrow. Our mother yelled and screamed at us constantly, and we could never do anything right. We watched each other get beaten with electrical extension cords. While we were being beaten, mom Beulah showed no remorse. She had a hateful, "I can't stand your presence" demeanor. Each one of us shivered in fear of our next emotional massacre. When she wasn't screaming or beating us, mom Beulah was distant and emotionless. You could not read her at all.

My siblings and I lived in daily terror and on the verge of panic, as we never knew when this human volcano was going to pour hot lava words and/or actions, leaving us with third-degree psychological burns that would penetrate our being and damage us for a lifetime. I was diagnosed with Post Traumatic Stress Disorder (PTSD) at a late age, because I continued to sabotage myself without any good reason long after correcting much of my life. My counselor, Dr. Pamela Thompson gave me the tools to heal my PTSD and I rose to a new heights; kudos to therapy.

My double life began early, as sitting in my elementary school classroom was such a welcomed contrast, to what it was like to live in my three-room house. In school when given an assignment, I could pay attention, complete it and receive the highest grade possible: A+! It took my mind off that lonely, hollow place that I knew I had to return to at the end of the school day. A sadness bubble, bigger than life, surrounded my body when at the end of the school day, the bell rang. Only loneliness and misery awaited me as I began my trail of fear home.

Nonetheless, I sat in my happy space at school, where teachers and school work was a joy. One typical day in my sixth grade class, I, without notice or explanation, heard my name called to be moved to the "A" class. Probably any other child would have seen this as a good thing. Of course, with my background, I internalized it as rejection. I was utterly devastated. It was well past my prime into my adulthood that I realized it was a great accomplishment. But at the time, being in this new classroom setting was very traumatizing to me. I didn't know any of the students in this class, and felt vastly different and below inferior to them even though I made a few friends, which helped to ease the discomfort. For the most part, I was on pins and needles daily—yet I was compliant, following all the rules my teachers required. I had a few mishaps with my classmates, even though I tried to be pleasant.

From the fifth grade to the seventh grade, I did my best not to draw attention to myself. Some of my friends always talked about their boyfriends, so I wanted to fit in, and say that I also had a boyfriend. My brothers Kenneth and Billie Rank said I was black, ugly, fat, and bald-headed. So I thought I should pick out the ugliest boy in the seventh grade and tell everybody that he was my boyfriend, and maybe, just maybe, he would like me back. An ugly girl gets the ugly boy. Two not-so-pretty people falling in love sounded reasonable to me. I picked a boy named JD...uuuuuuuugggglyyy like me...or so I thought.

I was wrong. Once again, the merry-go-round ride of getting publicly blasted found its way into my already dark existence. As I walked home from school with my girl playmates, I was blindsided by this hostile, verbally violent boy named JD. He started ranting and raging razor-blade remarks at me in front of my playmates. Rippling shame waves went through my body as he confronted and ripped away my made up fantasy relationship lie. I just ignored him and kept my eyes to the ground. He said, "Why are you going around telling everybody that I am your boyfriend? I would never have anyone as ugly as you. You're fat, ugly and don't have any hair. Your dress looks like something out of a landfill. Don't you ever tell that lie on me. You embarrassed the shit out of me. I hate you!"

Caught red-handed, I just remained quiet and kept walking. Damn, I was busted. He had rejected my indirect request, and he did it publicly, in the presence of my "A-class" buddies. Many of my friends had said they had a boyfriend and I lied that I had a boyfriend too trying to please and fit in with the crowd. I was desperate for approval and had a paper thin sense of self-worth. I had a huge issue with what professionals later called, "people pleasing," starving for approval, even if it meant harming myself.

SEVEN PEOPLE, ONE BATHROOM

Getting ready for school was troublesome like so many parts of my young life considering everything that was going on in my home; I was terrified to take a full bath. And one sad day, it all came crashing down on me. Going to that one bathroom was like walking to my own execution—I wasn't sure if I would come out alive. The thought of fighting off those brothers of mine was mind blowing. I had no one to tell; I endured all of this terror alone. I was made to feel like I was in a concentration camp, with death being a welcomed way out.

    The effect of these living conditions bled over into the other areas of my childhood life. I was always late for school because I wanted to avoid my siblings in the morning. I had no one to protect me as I bathed, so I did not bathe often. In my childish mind, I thought my hygiene could be like my brothers; however, I learned quickly that this definitely was not going to work for a girl. We require daily baths and fresh undies.

    I did not have enough underwear, and worse than that, I had no place to wash and hang them out, without fear that it would create poor conduct from my two mean brothers. The chaos of this situation exceeded all limits one sunny day. Some girls and I were on the playground. We played and then sat down. All of a sudden, one girl started kicking at my feet which caused me to move my closed legs. A "Thriller" Michael Jackson stench seeped out, as my underwear was dirty, and I had not washed for days. Even I was aware of the funk. I hung my head in deep shame. My grandmother had always told me to wash and change my undergarments daily; I wanted my mother to tell me that, but she never tried to instruct or guide me. As a result, I didn't do what Grandma said out of rebellion;

heck, she was old to me. What she said didn't count. Besides, she wasn't my mother! I really relate to NeNe Leakes of the Atlanta Housewives TV Show. She carried so much pain from knowing her mother kept some of her children but sent her away to live with her grandmother. Man oh man, that tears the insides of a child to shreds, leaving them fragmented and deeply bruised.

I used to daydream about my mother buying me seven pair of colorful girl underwear, and she would spend time with me to make sure that things were washed and ready for the week. That never happened. Much of my young life was spent learning how to take care of myself. Today one of my favorite hobbies is taking a spa bath with fun fragrances and having lots and lots and lots of fresh lady garments. I don't take a well-stocked bathroom for granted nor a dresser drawer of my very own full of briefs; amazing grace, a far cry from the playground disaster.

Apparently, the girls told my teacher about the humiliating incident on the playground. She turned around and called my mom to inform her that I had come to school unclean. Later that night, my mother, who usually ignored me, quietly approached me and said softly, "Go take a bath, Bonita." She monitored our one bathroom that time, and I could take a bath without fear of being abused or harmed. She never had a conversation with me about the school calling or staying clean after that embarrassing day. We never addressed the issue again. I was pleased that she was nice about it.

I learned to take better care of myself on my own, so that I would never be humiliated in public like that again. Many years would evaporate before I knew I was worthy enough to bathe in luxury and have a truckload of clean undies. Poverty, neglect, a dysfunctional family, alcoholism, undiagnosed family mental illness, and abuse can leave a mountaintop of unintentional damage. It can take years to unearth and discard. Some people never recover. It pains me greatly today to see my mom and three remaining siblings continuing to live in earth's Hades.

Scarring Words

I avoided those trips to the bathroom to decrease my interactions with the two evil brothers: Billie Rank and Kenneth Lee. I would think about the battle sure to come and who would impose the most misery and escalating abuse upon Bonita. Will it be the mother Beulah, Billie Rank or Kenneth Lee? I clumsily tried to dodge the insults but with little success. "You are fat, ugly, and retarded," said my brother Billie Rank. Then, my brother Kenneth chimed in with, "You are the ugliest girl in the "A" class. Compared to the other girls, Michelle Morgan and Harriett Strickland (the pretty girls), you are *ugly*! You don't have any hair, bald-head, skanky, ugly, fat unwanted witch. We both hate you!"

As usual, I froze and didn't make one comeback crack. I just ignored them and walked away. Somehow I knew what they had said about me was a bunch of lies, *filled with hate*! "DON'T NEED NO HATE A RATION, CELEBRATING NO MORE DRAMA IN OUR LIVES, WE DON'T NEED NO HATERS", by Mary J Blige expresses it wonderfully, Thanks Mary! Hell, I was smart in school, and my grandmother thought I was special, and so did my teachers. Nothing felt quite as splendid as straight "A"s on my report card. Say what you want about me, because at that time I had already decided to go to college some day! I kept quiet to de-escalate their scarring words, and somehow endured the torture. It was as if some magical power was protecting me. I never became mean-spirited or dignified their abuse with abuse. However, I was sometimes mean to my younger sister and brother for no good reason—hurt people hurt other people, and healed people heal other people.

Occasionally, I hurled a defensive word or two, like "trunk nose," "shut up," "jerk," or "kiss my grits." Otherwise, I loved to save my energy for intellectual encounters, since it depleted easily. Later on in life, I learned I am an introvert. Giving my energy to others involuntarily happens minute by minute to me, as involuntary as a human's heartbeat. I required rest and bunches of time to regroup.

Being emotionally violated by two of my four brothers was routine in my economically disadvantage home. I became completely conditioned to being insulted, neglected and passed around like a victim of verbal rape, and emotional violence. I survived what would have trampled most people, according to several therapists, as well as several spiritual teachers. Somehow, I found a self-driven push to find my authentic self at all costs!

Somewhere in the cells of my body, in my DNA, I was directed to press on, in spite of the mind-blowing agony that existed in my family. As a matter of fact, I was so familiar with torment that I continued to manifest it, long after I left home.

The Ten Commandments Movie

My favorite escape from the gloomy, cutting uncertainty in my home was a great movie on Saturdays at our neighborhood theater on Hunter Street. My elementary school, one block from Washington High School, routinely passed out free tickets to the nearby Ashby Street Theatre, a few blocks from my elementary school! It's truly strange that out of all of the movies I saw at the Ashby Street theatre with my brothers and sister, there is only one movie I remember. This one resonated with my soul and inner-most being: *The Ten Commandments*, starring Charlton Heston. It beckoned to me like a coastal lighthouse does for approaching ships, guiding them safely to shore.

My eyes stared at the screen as I felt volts of electricity shoot through my body. I was on fire in a way that I had never experienced before. What was it about this movie that awakened every strand of my DNA? I was mesmerized...something was turned on that day that would be the guiding theme for the fabric of my life. I realized that there was more to this miserable, painful life that I was born into on, *ugh*, 280 Chestnut Street! Bigger than that, more magnificent, I ascertained that there is a powerful God who can turn the most horrendous situation into a thing of beauty. I'd received a wordless knowing I later learned is called discernment.

I felt a deep connection with Moses, barely escaping death, misunderstood by his new family, hating injustices, being exiled by the only family he knew, torn down, stripped of his greatness, being born on the other side of the tracks, and the beat goes on. I never forgot that movie. It was the light force that I would be inching toward the rest of my life. It gave me an answer to my disturbing "home life" existence. There, on that day, that very glorious day, my personal quest for God began, but it would take years and years before this affect could be seen on me by anyone—even me. It was more like an underlying current—quiet, powerful and very present. It was the gas in my human car body—my fuel! Like Moses in the movie, who dealt with forced abandonment, slave to prince, and prince to exile, and finally exile to God's leading man, my life had many unexpected twists and turns as well.

As the daily trauma in my young life continued, the memory of this movie would fade into the background and practically disappeared. My mom still took her frustrations out on us six kids, and the merciless beatings continued. Nothing changed. The house I lived in was as awful as it was before this soul-satisfying movie dropped into my world. Sometimes I shivered in this worse-than-death life. I knew nothing about suicide which would have relieved me of this pain. Years later my brother Kenneth completed his suicide, which broke all of my denial and my minimizing of the corrupted experience at the hands of mom Beulah.

Even though things were still pitch-black, I caught a glimmer of hope after taking in this movie. I often dared to think that maybe, just maybe, this great strong power could help me. This wonderful source of love who saved Moses from being assassinated at birth, favored by a family member of the enemy, and raised as a prince could give me help, too! Moses escaped death by Pharaoh, was exiled into the desert, and survived—what a coincidence—only to return to Egypt years later to confront Pharaoh Ramesses, the son of Seth, who was then the new Pharaoh. Moses requested that Ramesses release the Hebrews from bondage, but he refused. What a magnificent story: it soothed my mind.

My favorite part, which is forever etched into my psyche, is when Moses gets to the Red Sea, and it appears that he and the other Hebrews are doomed. Wow. I connected with that with an intense focus. Heck, I felt doomed to pain and suffering with no way out of my frightful day-to-day nightmare. Mom Beulah and my mean siblings had me trapped, smothered in abuse, hate and poverty. I did not know that God was setting things in motion for me to not only *Survive* but inch by inch to heal and *Thrive*.

So here is Moses, at the cliff of the Red Sea, and Pharaoh's army is advancing, and my God, my God does his miraculous thing and parts the Red Sea! A smile appeared, way down deep inside of me, and a fierce determination to withstand anything was unleashed. I carried this extraordinary spark of strength within me from that very important day forward, which would prove to be my saving grace. Reflecting back, this source of inner strength and direction was birthed that day, and has remained with me *from the day of that movie, to the present.*

Unfortunately, over the years, I developed a slight amnesia, and the effect of this film was forgotten and dormant, but it was nevertheless, present. I didn't know how to use it or access it, because this guidepost was buried under layers of heartbreak until many moons later, when I entered the doors of spirituality groups in conjunction with Unity New Thought Christianity. This turned out to be a powerful combination.

BEULAH: AN EQUAL OPPORTUNITY ABUSER

After my awesome movie adventure, I returned home feeling sad, lonely and scared. I crawled into my bed and went to sleep. "Bang, bang, bang!" Loud echoing sounds bounced off my ears as I jumped from a restful night of sleep. I slept on a roll-away bed that had metal wires to hold the mattress beneath me. The only good thing about this roll-away bed was that I could at least lie down and sleep.

My little hands quivered with terror as I ran them across my eyes. What the freak is going on now? I thought to myself -can't a kid have some peace in her sleep? No. Remember? You are a member of *The Addams Family*—mysterious and kooky was the norm for us.

This man, my mom's boyfriend at the time, moved in slow, backwards, gliding steps. I expected to see flesh splattered as he strolled backward into my pretend, fake bedroom, and I mean authentically fake. It had a sink, stove, refrigerator, table and chairs, cabinets full of government groceries, and, to my dismay, my roll-away bed was also where my sister slept when she wasn't in the forbidden to me Queendom room with my mom Beulah. More times than not, my sister slept in my mother's "better than thou" bedroom, also known as "the locked living room."

Just as quick as I was startled out of my sleep by the sounds of the gunshot blasts, mom Beulah—still with the gun in her hand while her boyfriend was fleeing from her attack. They stopped the gun fight and she and her boyfriend regained their composure and returned to her castle-like room.

I resumed my fade-into-the-background posture, in my corner, dungeon-like bedroom/kitchen area, in despair. She never spoke of the shooting incident, and I dared not ask. I learned to just suck it up and pretend it wasn't real, like nothing had ever happened. No one got shot; no blood was ever seen. They must have been blank bullets—sure didn't sound like it though!

Throughout my life, this scene was repeated by mom Beulah over and over again. It first reappeared when my oldest brother, Danny, had a big argument with her. Mom Beulah anger skyrocketed to her pulling out a gun and putting it to his head, saying, "I'll kill your goddamn ass—I'm the Mother!"

Thankfully she didn't shoot the gun, and he drove off. Forty years would pass before Danny, my brother, would speak to her, and he was near death at the time. We all missed him so, because he was our step-in father as well as our step in mother during our growing up years. I barely saw him after age 16. I didn't know until I was well into my forties that both my brother Danny and mother Beulah had an undiagnosed mental illness called schizophrenia that comes in a spectrum of levels from mild to severe.

A *Healthcare Professional* gave me the family diagnosis after I contacted them because Debbie and Kenneth were both exhibiting unstable behaviors at home. The health professional came to our home and made the diagnosis.

Masking the Pain

I coped as best I could with Mom Beulah but she knew how to shut me down by yelling; she was a screamer. So I dared not to ask questions or make comments about anything, because she just screamed ugly words of contempt. So there was never a dialogue about what happened that day—the day she shot at her boyfriend. But I knew what I saw, and I knew what I'd heard.

With me being naturally kind and tender-hearted, my coping mechanism was to sink into a self-made shell. Years later, when I finally went to therapy about my many struggles, my first therapist told me that I was an empty shell on the inside. Life in that house with Beulah and five other siblings had gutted and rotted out my insides. It was vacant; anything or anyone could come and take up residence there.

My escape was to hide, become invisible, and mask the pain by eating anything I could get my hands on. Most of the time, it was beans and cornbread (government groceries). This cycle of overeating and abuse was repeated countless times, and as a result, I became a compulsive overeater—a person who must eat the whole cake, bag, or carton of whatever food item I saw. It makes sense now. I was trying to fill up my insides, which had been removed, slashed away by emotional neglect.

To add more misery to my state of affairs, I became the only fat child out of six siblings. What in the hell did I do that for? It gave two of my brothers yet another reason to badger me to emotional death for the remainder of my childhood. I would have done anything within moral reason to quiet the bully attacks. I hid from them and ate more than ever to kill the monster of terror that became my powerful, invisible demon that haunted me for years.

Even when my siblings weren't around, this scary force talked to me, and influenced me to do things no person in their right mind would do! It was cunning, powerful and baffling. *The Exorcist* demon and my eating disorder seemed to be ruled by the same evil.

I lived with several demonic forces, and they all attached themselves to me. It was like a scene in the movie *The Mummy*, with all the bugs crawling into my skin, slowly taking over my body. I was reduced to the living dead—yes, dead woman walking. The light in my eyes flickered out—I merely existed from then on. Cramming food down my throat had me by the horns...I was doomed! I subconsciously acted out every chance I got with food and once I started dating, I acted out with men. The "crazy flight" found me and landed on the runway of my life, destined for a crash with no survivors. The human spirit can only take so much *pain* before it collapses.

Sitting and thinking about my life's travels I realized that I had lost a big chunk of Bonita. I shared some parts of my story in my latter years with my spiritual accountability partner, and she said to me, "Bonita, it's a wonder you didn't blow your brains out." Up until then, I'd minimized my pain in order to cope; but it poured out in various addictions.

Hey, Fat Girl!
This overeating thing had me handcuffed by the wrists. I felt like a burden to my family. So I turned to food and developed an eating disorder. I starved and binged to silence my pain. Becoming a compulsive overeater buffered the cycle of abuse that occurred repeatedly.

With large bags of food, I hid from them and ate more and more food to kill the monster of terror. Watch out—I stole food from anywhere! And if asked if I knew what happened to a particular food, my answer was always, "I have no idea." Yet my weight spiraled upward, almost as fast as the speed of sound.

I recall returning to school from summer break, and while in the lunch line, out of the blue, the school custodian made the comment, "she has gained so much weight over the summer!" He continued to make statements, but I was so embarrassed that his words faded into mere muffled sounds.

This really hurt because I secretly had a crush on him. He was tall and drove a nice car and, I felt he and I had something in common. People were always judging you externally—what you look like, what you weigh, your type of job, the length of your hair, the shade of your skin and so forth. I had an attraction to others not considered popular—the ones people treated poorly. Mr. Mike, our school janitor, was judged by his job. I thought that was so dumb…we are all important; even me despite my appearance and my zip code. Mr. Mike could have kept his criticism to himself!

Even so, going to school was a welcomed time so different from the daily nightmare at home. At school, there were procedures, rituals and routines. From 8:00 a.m. to 3:00 p.m., I knew I would be safe and away from my Freddy Krueger brothers, and my *Addams* and *The Munster's Family* environment. Living in the household was like having all of those fictional television series occurring simultaneously. I kept hoping that one day I would wake up and realize it was all a bad dream. Unfortunately, it didn't happen. So I turned to food over and over again—it was my only way out. When I first tasted cream cookies, they were a hit. My insides did a MJ moonwalk, and I felt an insatiable high. I knew at that instant that I had found something incredibly satisfying. Little did I know it was going to be the beginning of a *second* hell. How does one go to hell twice in a lifetime? I don't know how, but I did.

Over the years, my food addiction spiraled completely out of control. I was an addict. When my body craved a fix, I was defenseless, similar to a vampire's thirst for blood. I started working at age 16, and with money to buy food, I was off to the races. I had to have fried chicken, mashed potatoes with gravy, biscuits with butter and honey, chocolate chip cookies, half a gallon of ice cream, a 3 Musketeers candy bar, a Kit Kat bar, and finally, a large bag of potato chips. Then I'd wash it all down with a liter of diet coke. I had to satisfy this urge—stronger than logic, intellect or self-will—so I found myself doing whatever it took to get my food binge on. One hour after the first eating binge, I was ready to jam more large quantities of food down my throat again. I had to have honey buns, M&M's, Oreos, cake, pie, doughnuts, a Big Mac meal, and as usual, a diet coke to wash it all down.

Getting My Food Fix

Before age 12, my chances of getting my hands on store-bought food were slim to none. And wouldn't you know it: my addiction preferred junk food from the corner store. The owner was Mr. Bass—a kind and friendly guy. My grandmother, Mary Lancaster, would give us kids a nickel, a dime or a quarter when we completed a chore. With that money, I zoomed to Mr. Bass's supermarket to purchase my favorite items: a pack of five cookies, Metropolitan ice milk and a candy bar. If I only had a dime, I would buy ten Mary Jane candies—heaven on earth, foodgasm, y'all! The only problem with this method was that I couldn't keep my fix going. I needed a flow of money to quiet my obsession with food.

Then one day, one great day, my life changed, and I welcomed it with open arms. Mrs. Beavers asked me to go to the corner store to pick up her grocery order. The next thing she said stopped me in my tracks: "I'll pay you, honey, with twenty-five double stack cream cookies (25 cents), and you can choose your flavor." I quickly ran her errands, gave Mrs. Beavers her items, and rushed to be alone with my newfound friends: sugar and junk food. In order not to share my cookies, I hid under our house, which stood on tall bricks. I opened the bag and looked inside at my cookies.

I slid one over my tongue and licked the white cream, followed by the crunchy smooth bites of the two cookies, which together equaled one of my twenty-five cookies. I spent the rest of the day doing this, one by one until all twenty-five cookies were gone. I had crossed the line and stepped into the twilight zone of an eating disorder. I just called it ED (Eating Disorder)! Bring on the cookies, cake, candy bars and ice cream. Heck, while I was bingeing, there was no mom Beulah, mean brothers or a 280 Chestnut Street: it was only pure pleasure—a needed get away from my mounting pain! Like the movie, *A Beautiful Mind*, starring Russell Crowe, my eating disorder became a visible, real, living thing, convincing me over and over to succumb to its demands.

WHAT IS MY NAME?

Another heartbreak besides the ones already mentioned is the story I learned about my name. No child wants to hear from their mother that his or her name was spelled wrong. Somewhere in the daily routine of living in the same house, mom Beulah, with much disagreement, stated that the nurse at the hospital had spelled my name wrong. While listening to her, I thought to myself, "Why didn't you just go to the hospital and have my name corrected?" I felt like I didn't mean much to her, I knew what was in her mind: "Oh, it's not that important. It's just *her*, the unimportant daughter."

This story really messed with my head. It was inconceivable to me that a nurse—a stranger—gave me my name when I was first born. It gave me a feeling of the child put in a basket and left on a stranger's porch—not wanted, abandoned by his or her mother, somewhat like Moses.

I was named Bonita Joyce Gay by a nurse and not my mother. It actually should have been "Bernita Joyce Gay." No one wants to be walking around in life with the wrong name. My name identity was damaged the day I was born, and this is a story she could have kept to herself. What child wants to hear, "Oh, you have the wrong name, and I never went back to fix it?"

So since my first day of life, I have been stuck with "Bonita." I had many rebellious tantrums and tried to spell it correctly as "Bernita." But my teachers would only change my name from "Bernita" to "Bonita." I was terrified to ask my mom to come to the school, talk with my teachers, and tell them the same story she had told me; I just visualized her going into her routine rage, as she often did at the drop of a hat. I finally concluded that if it was not important enough for my mother to correct my name legally, then I would learn to tolerate "Bonita."

Slowly, I began to accept my name and even to like it. In a sense, I felt better about it- at least the abuser (mom Beulah) didn't get to name me. With a flippant attitude, nose in the air, it was sort of freeing to get back at her—I got my punches in wherever or however I could. A stroke of luck, I'd say; one of my few charmed moments.

WITH FRIENDS LIKE THESE, WHO NEEDS ENEMIES(MEAN GIRLS)

After that failed stunt I pulled, JD the ugly boyfriend meets the ugly girlfriend dissolved. Looking back, I lived in a fear fog that controlled how I saw life. It never dawned on me until later that my fake friends from the "A" class had told JD about what I'd said, and arranged for him to meet us as we left the school building, heading toward Ashby Street. The brutal attack from JD yelling at me in front of my friends was just another reminder that I was human junk. "Call 1-800-Got-Junk"...we will remove your discarded items—even humans—for less." I wouldn't be so lucky! They'd probably return me to mom Beulah and her emotional penitentiary facility, called 280 Chestnut Street.

It took lots of time for me to come to terms with the fact that this was planned in advance; however, I was clueless before it happened and clueless after it happened due to my shadow demon called fear. I went into survivor mode: endless denial swept under the rug!

Being roasted was a common occurrence. So I minimized practically everything and dared to hope for love and acceptance someday...any day. And so a year later, on another particular day, I got an opportunity to belong...to *fit in*...Yes, Sir!

It was a beautiful late Spring Day. Birds were busily chirping, and to my delight I was about to get a much-needed break from my 280 Chestnut Street *House of Horrors*. Some classmates from my esteemed "A" class asked me—let me repeat this, *they asked me*—to go swimming with them. Since I longed to belong to a group, any group, I said yes with flash quickness. I was euphoric to have friends—at least I thought they were friends.

We talked in a friendly way as we walked to the neighborhood park. For some unknown reason to me, each of them was unusually nice to me. Being a trusting, naïve child, I didn't suspect a thing. I couldn't see it coming. I just felt happy and carefree; it radiated all over my body. I was in my zone, and I was beginning to transform into another person.

I lit up like a Christmas tree as we played at the pool together. "Bonita," Tonya said. "Come over here, near the deep part of the water." I shrugged my shoulders and replied, "Oh, no...I'm afraid. I have never been in a pool before."

I was elated just to be there with other girls from my "A" class. "They like me," seeped from between my lips. This is as good as it gets. I thought, "Wow!!! I finally have friends who genuinely care about me." I felt euphoric, warm and fuzzy. I wanted them to keep liking me. So I celebrated my newfound status by humming my favorite song, "I'm in with the in crowd, baby, so in touch with the in crowd." With a cockiness and newfound confidence, I allowed Patricia and Tonya to lure me to sit on the section of the wall between the shallow and the deep end of the pool.

Out of the blue, and without warning, Patricia snuck up from behind me, and with a force of a strong wind, she pushed me over into the deep waters of the pool. I shifted from heaven to hell within a matter of seconds. I had no idea I was being set up for a prank tease! A thousand layers of humiliation vibrated through my mind, body and soul, leading to negative thoughts that came to the forefront of my mind. I thought to myself, Bonita, how could you dare to think that someone, anyone, would really like you? Darn it GIRL, your daddy left you, your mom ignores you, and two of your brothers are ashamed to be seen in public with you. So what gave you the audacity to think anyone would consider you a real human being, a normal person? You are more like Norma and Norman from 'The Bates Hotel' TV series.

At the same time, I fought with all my might and all my strength to stop sinking to the bottom of the pool! While strokes and frantic struggles availed me of nothing, I continued to sink. Within moments that felt like forever, I knew I was going to die. I was drowning! My diligent efforts to get back to the top of the water proved to be unsuccessful.

In that instance, I also remember that I had sneaked off to the park without getting mom Beulah's permission. We never talked anyway. Forget asking her anything! She avoided me like the plague, and I avoided her in return. I didn't like being around her, and the feeling was mutual. I had shut down. She trained me well; her favorite scream was, "shut up!"

Panic struck and I became deeply afraid that mom Beulah would hear about me drowning at the park and re-kill my ass, because the family policy for me, and all of us, was to stay in the yard: the 280 Chestnut Street yard. We didn't have many major rules in my chaotic home; however, this was the big one—the ride-or-die one. If you broke a rule, minor or major, prepare yourself for the electrical extension cord beating. It was the worst form of physical abuse a child could ever experience.

All six of us "chilluns" walked around on egg shells. Following a beating was the only time we felt empathy for one another. Then, in a flash, we would block it out and return to business as usual, hurting each other. Hurt people hurt. Healed people heal—although with the exception of

Grandma Mary, there were no healers present. Kiss, kiss, kiss, hug, hug, hug to you, Grandma Mary.

Two new thoughts burst forth silencing all other thoughts. Thought one, "You are dead," came with a feeling of sadness and loss. Thought two, "stop fighting the water" came from an unknown source full of beauty, power and peace. I had no choice but to obey it and let go of the results; be it injury or death. My soul completely accepted the second thought … more specifically, the voice.

These thoughts were rapid, like automatic machine guns. And don't forget: I'm descending to the bottom of the pool. I relaxed into it and trusted. All fear vanished. I felt safe and protected. There was an absence of the knowledge of life and death and a feeling of sheer peace…angelic peace…an agape lovingness…no worries, no cares, just joy, and then… poof, mystically, I was at the top of the water and I was able to find the division wall again that separated the deep from the shallow.

I wiped the water from my face and just decided to go home. I looked forward to the familiar kitchen/bedroom I had, and my roll-away bed and hot bowl of beans and tasty cornbread with butter. The concept of "mean girls" ain't nothing new: that day, that day, *that* day I almost drowned. This was a premeditated act by mean girls who pretended to like me. We shared the same sixth grade class every single day! And yet, they took advantage of my poverty and my neediness with callous hearts.

I felt the agonizing odor of betrayal; another tear in my cracked places grew. I sighed and wondered if I would ever fit in…would I ever wake up from this "daymare." As far as the voice that saved my life, preventing me from drowning, I could never erase it from my memory. At the same time, as always, I had no one to tell, so I bottled it up inside and kept it a secret until now.

My soul was reawakened that day. Once again, I knew hope and strength. My source of help had silently come to me…my quiet guide smoothed the waters to ensure my life did not end. Mom Beulah, or my five siblings, never knew about the pool attempted homicide in the form of dangerous child's horseplay. If one drop of it got back, I would have surely been beaten to near death by mom Beulah with her three-layer electrical extension cord for daring to leave the yard. The cords left swollen welts of skin all over your body.

Too bad for us kids in the 1960s because "child abuse" was an unknown topic of concern that no one talked about. The new generation has it good because now all kinds of child protection laws are on the books, probably because of what my generation endured.

GOOD TIMES WITH MOTHER BEULAH

Oh, yes. There were pleasant times with mother Beulah. She'd send us to the movies on Saturday, or she would orchestrate a family outing at Stone Mountain Park on the fourth of July. Happy times—the warmth of these rare and short-lived times felt like colorful rays of sunshine. I basked in them.

It was troublesome to enjoy these pleasant moments, because our overall relationship was filled with criticism, put-downs, and harsh demands. Most of the time, it was a complete deprivation of her presence. It was like an up-and-down swirling roller coaster ride. At any moment, I knew that something scary was waiting to engulf my very being. My insides shivered at the thought of the other, more frequent, mother Beulah returning. This household living condition produced what the therapist diagnosed as "post-traumatic stress disorder." Untreated, it could destroy any attempt at having a functional life.

Somehow her gestures, these kind acts of mother Beulah, relayed the message to me that she was, indeed, attempting to be a good parent. Perhaps she wasn't equipped with the necessary training or capacity to do anything different from what she was doing. Nonetheless, these few moments with her lightened the emotional blows that were sure to come to us later. I'd say that 90 percent of the time, the six of us lived over a sinkhole to be swallowed in without warning!

Other attempts at sweet times were when she would extend friendship to me by calling me, "Bows," short for "Bonita." I would then force a frightened smile on my face, because I had come to learn that when she called me "Bows," she was trying to be nice to me. My brother Kenneth came to know what the nickname "Bows" meant, so he would call me "Bows" and coming from him, I would release a real smile, as he had no power to harm me. It was sort of like the Indian peace pipe—a ritual symbolizing a truce!

I used to daydream—oh no, make that *fantasize*—about coming home one day to find that moment mother Beulah had snapped out of this badness, or whatever you want to call it. Surely this misery was going to end, and to help it along, I often visualized myself arriving home from elementary school, finding mom Beulah waiting for me as I walked through the kitchen door. She would say in my fantasy, "Surprise! Surprise, Bonita; it was a long, cruel joke, and I'm sorry."

We'd hug, and I'd say, "Thank you, Mommy. Thank you for finally ending this nightmare, because I was just about to lose my mind up in here. Oh, Mother; it's finally over! Turn up, turn up!" My mind was similar to the Alfred Hitchcock character Norman Bates' psycho mind, now in the remake called "Bates Motel." Drifting in and out of reality, I'd dream up these things just to smile.

Needless to say, none of this ever happened, except in my mind. Instead, I continued to drag myself around, mustering up the will each day to bathe myself clothe myself, feed myself, and defend myself, in an effort to keep my sanity. I would go back to my one legal pain killer; crawling under our house and laying face-up, flat on my back, and eating my 25 cream-filled cookies. Forget you, world. I had earned my *crack food* money from "The Cat Lady," Ms. Beavers, who had what seemed like 15 cats, and as a result she always needed cat food from the corner store, as well as other things. She would pay me in cookies and any other kind of food which deadened my lonely and neglected feelings.

Part Two: Pre-Teen to College Life

"No man can justly censure or condemn another, because no man truly knows another."

Sir Thomas Browne,
"The Evils of Child Abuse and Neglect"

GOOD-BYE GRADE SCHOOL, HELLO HIGH SCHOOL!
I survived the top class for two years and graduated to junior high school. So long E.R. Carter Elementary school!!! Woo hoo!!! Hello, High School!! Central Junior High School only had one grade level: eighth grade. I got a chance to start over—the slate was wiped clean. And a new chapter began. For the first time, all my teachers liked me, and also I made good friends with other students. My favorite teacher taught Russian, and she and I pledged to go on a diet together. This was my first attempt at controlling my weight. This dieting attempt went on and off several times, but by the end of the ninth grade, I had slimmed down considerably, and it felt great. And so emerged my second addiction: *romance*!

Having a boyfriend became more important than my first obsession, which was junk food, sweet food, crunchy food, fried food, and scrumptious anything food. Little did I know any addiction is a downward spiral to the underworld, be it food, romance, drugs, alcohol, shopping or spending; it all masked buried trauma and pain that must be dealt with—otherwise, it deals with you.

High school was pretty uneventful. Mom Beulah now had a car and opened her own business as a Hair Stylist. We moved into a house that had two levels. I had a real bedroom for the first time in my life. I shared it with Debbie. This new house had a full living room, dining room and kitchen, a screened porch, a backyard and yes….oh yes – a separate basement area with three rooms! Glory, Glory – for my brothers to live! Also for the first time we went to separate schools. They remained at Washington H.S. whereby I transferred to Frederick Douglas H.S. My life changed for the better. I did not have to deal with Billie Rank bullying me anymore. He was the wickedest of all my five siblings. He thrived in darkness similar to mom Beulah. Both were constantly attempting to poison my chances of happiness. They are definitely blood kin. Regardless, I blossomed, made friends and even became a member of the

"Who's Who Among American High School Students" publications in my junior and senior years for my scholarly achievements.

High School: My First Boyfriend

I thought this day would never come. I was seventeen and in the twelfth grade. Yeah! I had arrived…let's send up a thousand balloons, toot the horns, and ring the bells. I was a high school senior. I could say goodbye to mother Beulah and hello to success. Let me show you how life is to be lived! Yes, I'm going to get married, one; complete college, two; get a good job, three; buy a house, four; have a kid or two, five; and I'll be happy for once in my life! Or, so I thought. My newly found independence, ripe with fresh naïveté, gave me a false sense of confidence and self-reliance.

I was gung ho to enter the dating phase. Mom Beulah was cool with me dating at age 16 in my junior year in high school. Then, I fell hard; his name was Earl, and he was tall, dark and handsome. It was love at first sight for me. Earl was 24 years old, and I was 17. He lived with his female cousin and her son in an apartment. My new and perfect guy was a friend of my best friend, Barbara, who lived in public housing (Bowen Homes, now demolished). So since he was a friend of hers, I felt it was Okay to date him. I started sneaking out of the house to be with him and eventually slept with him. Boy, did I dislike sex—it was nothing like they said it would be! Now I know it's because he was a bad guy. Honestly, it was awful, but I knew that's what men liked, so I just played along. All I really wanted was to be held, caressed and loved—still looking for that hug and fatherly love from my absent dad.

Maybe if I had that father hug need fulfilled first, then sex would have been great, like God had created it to be. But I had no information. All I had was my fantasy mind, so I continued to go through life wearing blinders. I had no idea of normalcy. My life experience was skewed; so yes, my first experience with sex was disappointing and flat. Where the hell is the parade? The fireworks? I sure as heck didn't feel any. YUCK!!!

But I'm getting ahead of myself. Nonetheless, Earl and I became serious, and when I started to stay out all night, mother Beulah threatened to slam me with a cast iron frying pan if I stayed out again. She lifted her hand with that black iron pan in it, and I knew right then and there that I would go live with Earl. Damn her! I had had enough of her hurtful talk, abuse and behavior—17 years of it, to be exact. Little did I know that I was about to enter into the gates of hell number two with Mr. Earl. I moved in with him. I expected Earl to be my prince in shining armor. I persuaded myself that this new life would bring me the happiness I hungered for so intensely. To my dismay, the bottom of my life dropped even further, if that's possible.

My first grown-up attempt to better my life landed me in a public housing facility called *Capital Homes* on Memorial Drive in Atlanta, Georgia. These red brick apartments were crammed tightly together, with a small outside yard; so small that if you took one footstep, you'd miss it. I arrived home from school around four o'clock, and Earl's great-aunt would have a big pot of soup and cornbread ready. The smell of that soup warmed my insides within minutes. I managed to serve myself a bowl while relaxing at the dinner table. Soon Earl would arrive home from work, all fidgety and agitated, and the fight would start.

Questions began to roll out of his mouth. "What did you do when you got home?" I told him I ate some soup and sat around, trying not to bother anyone. Then he shouted, "Well, you need to do more! Hell! Shit! Do some chores." I thought to myself, "Hell! Shit! That's why I left home!"

My mom always bitched about us doing chores. "I'm not doing chores anymore. Got that, you son of a bitch?" Then wham, bang. The fight was on. I had spent my early years doing chores in two houses (my mom's and my grandmother's), and I'll be damned if I'm going to resume the maid role in this house of strangers. At least 12 people rotated in and out of our one-bedroom, subsidized apartment. It was Great-Aunt Sadie's apartment, yet adult relatives with their children were constant traffic, day after day.

Earl and I began to fight regularly. Words of anger were flung back at him, and on occasion, I would go back home to my mom. Once I cooled off, the compulsion to feel valued, wanted and loved sprung forth. I was thrust into a cycle of arguing, returning to mom's home, and then showing back up at Earl's place. This went on for months and became progressively worse. In between the chaos, the drive to get up and ride the bus to school was second nature. I always felt successful performing in my classes. I continued to be an honor student without much effort. School came so easy, I loved it! When I thought it couldn't get any worse between Earl and me, it did.

One day we started to argue, as usual. He asked me where I'd been, and I answered and said that I was at school. Earl replied, "You are a motherfucking lie, bitch. I told you to clean this damn apartment and cook. You can't just eat and sleep here."

I asked him, "Why not?" I wasn't bothering anybody. Obviously, this was how the family dynamics work: talk with the people you live with, ask for what you need, and share the chores. All of which I later evolved into as a result of my self-chosen personal growth journey, but at 17, I did not have a hint of *quality of behavior*; I simply imitated what I saw on 280 Chestnut Street. Plus, Earl drank too much and smoked marijuana. In the middle of me saying, "I ain't gonna do crap," a fist came slamming into my mouth. I grabbed my mouth in horror. Blood was everywhere. I began to cry, and mentally spun into a dark silence. I isolated myself from Earl that day, and I knew immediately that I would begin to end this relationship.

My first love became a bigger nightmare than this family of mine. They never took their fists out and hammered them into my mouth. My self-worth plummeted to an all-time low. Approximately one-third of my front tooth broke instantly from the impact of that punch to my face. I began to work myself out of this union. However, he and I made countless attempts to save us. As an apology, Earl paid to have my tooth repaired. Since gold crowns were popular in the 1970s, I chose a crown which I later regretted as it had to be redone every ten years until there no tooth left for a crown. Now sits an implant!!!

Things between us would be good for a few days but then return to the usual way. He swore he would never hit me again and he didn't. Instead, what he chose to do next was much worse. Now, whenever we argued, he threatened to kill me with a gun. Neighbors and relatives tried to help me. They would all warn me by saying, "Don't go back to his apartment, Bonita. Earl has a gun, and he has told everyone he's going to kill you."

My undiagnosed relationship addiction took over, and I was powerless to resist the urge to be in a relationship with him. In some hypnotic state, I would return to Earl and the one-bedroom, government project apartment with twelve relatives.

Within minutes, Earl appeared at the apartment. Neighbors and relatives shouted, "Run, Bonita! Leave this place now, because Earl bought a shotgun, and it's loaded. He's on his way to shoot you." Love addiction enticed me into wanting to make up with him. I loved him. I missed him. I felt so empty when we were apart. The threat of death wasn't even powerful enough to break the shackles of my relationship addiction. Earl caught up with me. We had a face off, and he had a loaded shotgun. I looked at it; he raised it up, and I closed my eyes, as I was prepared to die. I imagined that I heard a loud "kaboom"—those seconds seemed like an eternity. I stood there, waiting for the bullets to enter my body. Looking back, I had a silent death wish like my brothers and sister! My only hope in changing was that I met a man, and we would be good to each other, and we'd successfully master life! After a few seconds, I opened my eyes, and I was still alive. He didn't pull the trigger…Jesus saves! Yes, I was in deep trouble, unable to find peace or happiness anywhere. A second earlier, I had just faced death by a shotgun. Weary, confused and unsettled, I made a life-changing decision: I decided to go home to mom Beulah and tell her that Earl said to others and to me that he was going to kill me because of the arguing and fighting. All I felt was a terribly strong desire to be "loosed" from this destructive relationship. Even with all that drama Earl and I stayed together the night of the shooting scare and somehow blocked out the events of the evening.

Earl did not know that I was ready to make a change in my life. *Woman in the Mirror!* I arose early the next morning, gathered my things, and pretended to be preparing to go to school. I safely left Capital Home projects for the last time. I felt better just knowing I was free of Earl.

It was a Wednesday—one day after the shotgun incident at the apartment and I'm now at Frederick Douglass High School. Strange but true, I always had the capacity to attend school. Attending class was uneventful; all I could think of was going back to mom Beulah, and asking for help. Months earlier, I and my friend Barbara had gone to Grady Hospital's family planning clinic, and gotten on birth control. Getting pregnant was out of the question. I had goals and ambitions to fulfill. Slowly, the school day ended. I told mother Beulah that Earl had said that if I left him, he would kill me.

I was frightened of her possible reaction to this violent news, but I told her anyway. I had reached my bottom with this whole relationship thing!

Mother Beulah actually surprised me by giving me a solution to the whole Earl problem, which included several steps. I listened intently, for I had run out of answers on how to stay alive. I was waving in and out of a trance-like state, reliving the scene of Earl pointing the shotgun at me and firing. I corralled up the strength to stay focused on mother Beulah's plans. It was a strain to keep my mind on the conversation, but I did it for my own sake. Mother Beulah said, "I'll take you to school every day and pick you up as well. You will go to work with me at the salon on Saturdays." I became the shampoo girl. And lastly, I would take out a warrant on Earl for assault with a deadly weapon, and this time I was not going to drop it.

I had experienced what happens when you drop a warrant. I had taken out a warrant on Earl once before. I had told the police everything that had happened, and they prepared the warrant. Then the usual thing happened, I'd feel sympathy for Earl. Go to the police station and have the warrant dropped. The police got angry at me, and an officer looked me straight in the eye and said, "Bonita, are you telling me he didn't have a gun?" I said, "Yes, sir. He didn't have a gun." Within seconds, I heard him say, "Lock her up! That is perjury! 'You people' shouldn't come down here and waste our time by taking out warrants and then dropping them. Lock her up!" The second time he said it more harshly.

Thus, I sank lower than I ever imagined! Within minutes, I sat behind jail bars for the first time in my life. The shock of it all was too much for me, and I blacked out. Jail was for criminals. I was a high school honor student listed in the *Who's Who Among American High School Students* book in both my junior and senior years. Why weren't my smarts working now? This was the million dollar question that would eventually propel me out of darkness.

It became one of the *theme questions* running through the threads of my life. *Why weren't my smarts working in my personal life?* I always believed that if you are smart in school, you can be smart in life. I never accepted anything less. Intelligence was God-given, and I couldn't shake that, no matter what happened. Returning to this question, which was placed at the core of my being, was my invisible everyday counsel. I swallowed my pride and called mom Beulah, and I told her I was in jail. Within a few hours, I was released in her custody, with my upcoming court date in October of 1973.

I often relived that day of the loaded shotgun act not knowing how to process it. A great puzzle to be solved. I sifted through the events of my near death day again. Several of my friends, as well as Earl's friends and family members, caught up with me as my bizarre, driven-desire to see Earl overtook me. I faintly heard the voices of the well-meaning crowd as they urged me to turn around and seek refuge. The urge to see Earl again beckoned to me, even though I was warned repeatedly by my friends that Earl would make good on his death threat. He had purchased a shotgun and bullets and told everybody he was going to shoot and kill me upon my return.

I always returned to him. I was caught between two hells—hell at home with mom Beulah and siblings and hell with Earl—and Earl's hell seemed the lesser of the two. At least I'd be dead and out of pain. The thought of death was almost a relief...a reoccurring theme in my family. Years later, my second oldest brother committed suicide by police which means a person intentionally provokes law enforcement to shoot them. He did this by pointing an empty gun at an armed law officer. It happened at Grady Hospital in Atlanta in 1999. It was on the six o'clock news and in the local papers. With our upbringing my family members were destine to make the six o'clock news!

I continued to walk toward Earl's apartment. I was numbed, and faced death head-on. Suddenly, Earl stood in front of me with the loaded shotgun. We looked at each other, and no words were spoken. Anger engulfed his entire being as I had packed my bags and left him many days ago. I closed my eyes, and waited for death. After a few minutes, I opened my eyes and Earl had put down the shotgun. I began to weep. He embraced me and we walked silently to his aunt's apartment, where he and I had separate rooms. I shared the ladies' room, and he pretended to sleep on the sofa. We would meet in the middle of the night!

Intuitively, I knew that violence was not going to be in my love relationship. I didn't know much but emphatically knew that getting beat up and having my life threatened was a showstopper. Consequently, I permanently ended my relationship with Earl with the help of mom Beulah.

NEXT BOYFRIEND

Marching onward, some months later I resumed my pursuit of selecting Mr. Right, as I just knew I was Mrs. Right. However, I was wrong! The joke was on me! I was buried in denial which is not a river in Egypt and describes my thinking quite accurately. Surely finding a decent partner would be simple enough. All I had to do was, *select* a good guy. There was a flash of unsuccessful dates with Red and Jed. Next, there was William Ringfield, my second boyfriend. From this relationship, one child, my son Kornelius D. Ringfield was born.

I had mixed emotions about being pregnant because I expected it to happen after college, landing a job and after marriage. Nonetheless I embraced my mother —to- be status with pride. My revised plan was to give my child the best life possible by staying in college and getting into a secure career that I enjoyed.

Mr. Ringfield, did in fact want to get married. So I told mom Beulah that he would be coming to dinner the following Sunday for her blessings. She stayed away from the house that day instead of meeting with us. After that, William was difficult to deal with and said, "You'll never have a man as long as you listen to yo' momma!" That was the beginning of the end of our relationship.

My mom would not give Mr. Ringfield consent to marry me. Instead, she offered me her basement apartment and supported and encouraged me to finish college, which was one of her finest, most beautiful moments. No person is all bad!

My son's father and I disagreed a lot and had nothing in common, except volcanic flames of emotion. We did not get along. He was an ex-con and a street thief on drugs. I did not know this at the time. I was naïve, oblivious to the wicked ways of the street world.

I found the criminal lifestyle to be absolutely boring and just plain nonsense. Why would you break the law and risk spending time in prison? Why would you lie and serve harm on a platter to good people? No. The reality of the street world was, at best, for evil people. I was not buying the "street smarts" bull crap. Anyone can lie and steal and cheat.

These types of characters were wired differently from me. I just couldn't see the value in deceiving and hurting others. For sure, my DNA sent loud noises of, "I ain't with this." Along those lines, in a few months, I put distance between me and Mr. William Ringfield, but the same pattern as with Earl continued. We would make up and then break up. He wasn't changing nor was I.

I had my first son, and he was handsome and gave me a sense of direction. Determined to give him a better life was the catalyst that set my reconstruction in motion. I wanted to tame my life but had no knowledge of how to do it.

As I moved on again, I had another round of dates with Dennis, Shema, Keith, Gerald, Fred and Manny. Dating can be grim! I had now, at least, started dating college boys as I was a college student, too. However, I felt like an imposter, and lived in fear that someone was going to discover who I really was: "a nothing!"

My cells shouted to me, "You cannot ditch your 280 Chestnut Street family!" which left me feeling like battery acid had been tossed on me, and once again, I felt I was destined to live a crippled, dismantled, fearful life, one less than everybody else. Steering my way out of this road block was not going to be an easy or simple task.

COLLEGE LIFE

Men and college swirled around me simultaneously. Two years earlier, at age 18, I excitedly went off to Morris Brown College in Atlanta, Georgia. The college for the underdog! My circumstances and lack of healthy rearing put me at a high risk to fail; many individuals predicted my demise including brothers Billie Rank and Kenneth Lee! It was a few blocks from my childhood home on 280 Chestnut St. It was a fresh, new start in life, and I was steering the ship this time. So I was full of courage, and I had high hopes of turning my life around. Whew, Lordy, Lordy. My childhood was finally a done deal. What I'd failed to realize was that I had taken my pain with me. Growing up without my father's love or presence, I got into relationships with shady men, simply because they noticed me.

I had a hole in my soul as big as the Grand Canyon. I carried with me the assigned image of, "I am worthless dust." I was programmed to think I was less than zero, due to being called names, bullied, teased, screamed at, compared to others, and poor. I had no one to tell, no dad to tell, and a mother who didn't care. It was never Okay, just to be myself.

By the end of my freshman year, I had been abducted and raped by two men that were together, both criminals. "Wounded and childlike" described me quite well. I was too interested in the opposite sex due to my daddy issues. I desired and romanticized about an "honorable" relationship. I was confident that my academic strengths could be transferred to the realm of socialization. Psyche! Spoof! Gag!

Well, needless to say, things mounted up like trapped water behind a weak levee, and sooner or later, the levee broke. Unforeseen pressures were mounting, building, piling up, ready to spur a catastrophic explosion, madly devouring everything in its path…like me.

My friend Janet and I were freshmen at Morris Brown College. We were fresh meat to the world, trusting and innocent. After a long evening of class, studying and just hanging out, we met and headed for home on the Atlanta city bus. While waiting at the bus stop, a cute-as-all-get-out guy came up and asked me if I'd like a ride home. I smiled and sparkled on the inside like a Christmas tree on Christmas Eve. My genuine nature was to trust and to be good, and from that premise, I assumed most people were also that way. Here it goes again, Psyche! Spoof! Gag!

This guy and I went back and forth about accepting this ride. The more we discussed it, the more that I liked him, and the thought that Janet was with me boosted my confidence even more. So after a lengthy exchange, I said Okay, and Janet followed along reluctantly. I was a bad influence on her.

The cunning generational family curse of the absent, deadbeat dad was at work, and in full bloom. I remember clearly the phrase that put me in an involuntary, half-awake trance with this guy...of which I had zero strength to resist! This chocolate, sexy demon in disguise said to me, "Hey, relax. Trust me. Being with me is as safe as being with your daddy." Once the word "daddy" was stated, the spell was cast, and I followed him like a baby duck follows its mom. With this self-induced state, I thought, "Wow! My dad has returned after 16 long, agonizing years. Whew! Finally, I found the antidote to get him to come back to me."

Songs rang out sweetly in my head, "Daddy's home, daddy's home," and he's going to be so proud of me. I'm a honor student in college, and I'm a kind-hearted, good girl. All of these splendid scenarios played out in my head as Janet and I rode home with Mr. Sexy Chocolate. (By the way, he had a second guy who rode with us too. He just happened to leave that out during our intense persuasion dialogue.)

Everything was good, smooth and pleasant. The drive was comforting, and I embraced it with joy. It was a huge contrast to the cumbersome task of riding the city bus. Janet and I gave directions to her house, and before we knew it, we had arrived at her destination of home. We all waved good-bye. They had done as they said, so my confidence grew. I relaxed a bit, reduced my guard, but things took an awful turn for the worst. They did not follow my directions to my house. Instead, these two strange, demonic monsters started riding around, looking for a place to commit their crime. Immediately fear and terror rocketed through every vein in my body. I was about to be violated, or even killed.

Images of my mom and siblings flooded my mind. Even though my family was abnormal, it was the only thing I knew. I did not want to die like this, by the hands of two strange men I'd only known a few minutes. I felt terror, and then I went into shock.

Looking back, shock is a well-crafted defense mechanism, for without it, I would have panicked and flown into pure hysteria. Things would more than likely escalate, and my goal was to de-escalate and come out alive. I remained calm and protested with pleads, "Don't do this. This is not necessary." Sex without consent is horrific and psychologically damaging, and it pierces your soul like no other criminal act. No amount of pleading was getting through to these serpents of the night, and we finally hit the point of no return. This sick, diseased man stated with conviction that either I move to the back seat, or he'd take out his gun from the dashboard and shoot me. At that point, I had crossed into Rod Sterling's *Twilight Zone* and the classic TV series *The Outer Limits*—at once I was terrified and numb.

Full of tears and horror, I stopped fighting as he forced himself on me. "Dear God, I am being attacked by this fool," I thought. He demanded that I dare not scream or fight. I did not want to be shot if I could avoid it, so I complied. The other guy stayed quiet in the front seat. I had this vertigo episode, where things just went in circles, and I was spinning out of control. At that moment, I concluded that I would be dead fairly quickly, since neither man wore a mask.

Falling into a pit of hopelessness, I accepted death and decided that maybe it would be a hell of a lot better than the hell I'd lived through in the past flippant years. Shit, as I lay there, I said in my mind, "Just kill me and get this shit over with." Unable to be shocked anymore, it became clear that his friend was going to rape me too. I put up no resistance. Have your sex feast, and by golly, kill me and let me be free from this cruel-ass world. All I have ever known were wicked, evil, cruel-ass people anyway, so release me from this miserable planet.

Once both men satisfied their sexual appetites, I resumed my attempts to reason with them. I played it cool…no crying or pleading. I pretended I wasn't upset. I told them where I lived, and this time, they actually took me home. Thank God, I think they were rapists but not murderers! I secretly planned to get both of them arrested by acting like I wanted one of them to call me. My plan was to get their sorry, criminal asses to the police department. One of these stupid assholes did call me a little while after I got in the house.

My plan to lure him to law enforcement fell apart as I went to pieces and I cracked…I added another break to my already cracked psyche, alerting him to the fact that I was not Okay with his cruel actions, and he never called me again. My strength was at an all-time low that night!

A year or so later, our paths crossed once more. I was a cashier at a black-owned neighborhood store with predominantly black customers. It was small with well-stocked shelves. A customer came in and bought a few items. A young man with a large hat, dark, tall and medium built, approached the counter to pay for his food items. I had a flashback: memories of this jerk flickered through my mind. I had such hate and unresolved anger for him. For protection, Mr. Jones kept a loaded gun near the cash register. I glanced at the gun, and then I glanced at Mr. Asshole. I wanted *so* badly to empty that gun into his ass. Darn it, I just wasn't a killer—Ms. Soft-heart—and taking a life was something I just couldn't do. Even to this day, I can't hurt a fly. A wonderful supervisor, years later, said to me, "Bonita, there isn't a mean bone in your body!"

So with sadness, I rang up his purchases, all the while imagining his bloody, bullet-infested body falling to the floor. That day, I chose to move forward and let the karma of the universe handle this guy for his terrible injustices to me! His punishment is sure to come!

Thank you, colleague and supervisor Anita Lee-Willingham, for mirroring back to me one of my core personality traits. It would be years before I could embrace this part of myself, and even more years to attain the skills to be kind and caring, yet protect and take care of me. She and I are still friends today.

College life had many twists and turns. I was on my own much of the time and unaware that I was still carrying the ugly emotional garbage of my prior years. I had a part-time job at Burger King in north Atlanta. This job provided me with much needed spending money. On a fateful day, I clocked in as usual and began my shift. This night, I worked in the food-prep area. I began to bag some fries for an order, and suddenly, without warning, three armed men wearing masks came through the employees' door and pointed their guns at us. I stood there in shock, wondering if I would live or die.

"Stand still and do as we say, and nobody will get hurt," the robbers stated. I felt as if I were suspended in time, where seconds seemed like days upon days. My manager was told to lie down on the floor with his hands behind his back, and he complied. I was glad, yet disturbed at the same time, because in my mind flashed a heroic Superman, like the one out of the television scene, who would drop-kick the robbers, confiscate their guns, and single-handedly wrestle them to the floor with all six of their hands bound tightly. Fortunately, the reality of it was that my manager stayed calm and followed the robbers' orders, which ultimately saved all of our lives. De-escalating seemed to work with these new-age Billy the Kid lawbreakers.

The robbers stole all of the cash they could find. Next, at gun point, they put us, the employees, into the huge lock-in freezer. They then exited through the kitchen door into the customers' eating area and fired a few shots to indicate that they were serious. So we all waited and waited until we had enough courage to come out of the freezer. We resumed serving customers while my manager called the police to report the crime.

Emotional trauma was so deeply embedded in me that I just went on with my evening shift as if nothing happened and never spoke of it again, until now.

Luckily, I escaped an attempted second abduction and rape because I was armed(William Ringfield had brought me a gun) for my protection, survived an armed robbery at work, stolen food from employers, tried marijuana, and carried a gun to protect myself from dishonest men meanwhile, I was on the honor roll every semester.

To soothe myself, I binged on sweets and other foods. Uhmmm…what does this store have? Uh…everything!!! Okay…let her roll! Peanut M&M's, potato chips, Twinkies, Kit Kat bars, Oreo cookies and ice cream. It usually took me two to three days to come down off a "gain ten pounds" food binge. Overeating is how I dealt with life; life was the problem…binge-eating was my solution or so I thought. I twirled in a vicious cycle—food binge, life, food binge, life—my relief was a strict diet or diet pills. As the years passed, I lost the ability to control my weight and binge-eating.

Escape, escape…my addiction got so bad that I chose to have two boyfriends at the age of 19. One boyfriend for love and one for *the love of food was Okay*; player, player---lol. I was propositioned by my boss to be his mistress. He owned a food store, and it's no surprise that I chose to work there. Food, food, and mo' food! My "crack" food, my "weed" food—an eating disorder addict's paradise…I could eat whatever and how much I wanted, so for the first time, I considered such an offer.

Only an addiction could make you forget your morals. Satisfying that craving is *all* you can think about! The cravings must be quenched, or else you feel like walking into traffic. Exercising choice or having will power are both nil, erased by this illness.

I had repeatedly said, "No!" He was persistent. My flesh lost the battle when he laid all those credit cards in front of me. Suddenly, he wasn't so old, ugly and fat anymore. Addicts find ways to justify their actions. I was a fairly new single parent, sophomore in college, and my love boyfriend didn't offer me financial help. So somewhere in my self-talk, I convinced myself that the grocery store owner could be boyfriend number two (my love-of-food boyfriend)—it all made perfect sense to me!

My grocery store owner would pick me up in his sparkling new Cadillac, and we would hang out, shop, and play the kissing game. He showered me with money, and also gave me full use of his credit cards. All the while I was thinking, "Why do you think so much of the V?" I did not like being with either boyfriend. Women are so different from men- we need romance and security first, then and only then do we feel down with sexual healing.

He was happy blah, blah, blah is what I felt. I still wondered where the fireworks were that people talked about, 'cause I sure didn't see any in all this wasted hoopla. In fact, I was bored to death. Looking back, I had long since shut down all my emotions and was a walking vessel with no inner self…I was hollow! It was my defense mechanism in my box of survival tools.

This sick game was short-lived. Yes, I was an eating addict; yes, I wanted access to all the groceries I ever dreamt of; but the price was too high. Two dates and I was done. True enough, my self-esteem was low, but my moral code of conduct went into full gladiator mode. My Olivia Pope showed up in full attire, and demanded that I fix this! So, without one drop of sweat from my forehead, I said, "No, thank you… the end!" Of course, the next work day, I was fired.

My Professors

With my first pregnancy, Professor Jackson noticed my sadness and said to me, "You know, Bonita, lots of girls at Morris Brown College are having relations. They just didn't get caught. Cheer up! You're no less than any of them." Whenever he could, he'd give me a ride to college since he lived on my street. I took Psychology 101 from him. Another one of his popular sayings was, "Life doesn't begin until you're 40!" True dat, true dat! His words encouraged me to keep walking toward the light, out of my self-made brick road of gloom and doom! Mariah Carey's words in the song "Hero"...then a Hero comes along (Professor), with the strength to carry on; and you know you can survive. Lord knows dreams are hard to follow!!! Sometimes a song can be the best Therapy. YEAHHHH!!!

On the contrary, another one of my professors would openly put me down in class, and I was oblivious to it. A classmate had to call my attention to it, and then I became conscious of the insults and put-downs he openly hurled at me at any given moment. He'd make such comments as, "A student came to him and said I've gotten myself in trouble, he said she said to him, 'I've been bad.'" He was making fun of me and I didn't know it. I would sit at my desk (belly and all) and chuckle, because insults of that nature were foreign to me. He smiled and said it generally to the whole class. It didn't bother me, based on my history of abuse, but it bothered other students that he was behaving this way toward. Because much harsher words were used in my home, this situation made the professor's put-downs acceptable and largely mild in comparison. So him being judgmental, I thought, "Piece of cake—just give me my freakin' grade."

Well, he did: a "D." It was my first 'D' ever. I didn't give a damn; at least I'd passed. Reflecting back, I concluded that Professor Willis didn't like a pregnant girl attending college classes---I may have been the first one ever on that campus, it was 1975. Society had set rules at that time but I've never been a groupthink individual. Guess what? I didn't care. I loved college, learning and making good grades. It was my bliss. At that time, I didn't have a name for it, though. I just felt compelled to press forward—regardless of being pregnant or dysfunctional.

Relapse
Destructive cycles during my college years were the routine, the norm for me. Two years had passed, and many of my deficiencies reared their

ugly heads in my romantic relationships. And here I go again. Mr. Car Salesman asked if I had a boyfriend. I lied and said no. "Can we have a date?" he asked. "Well," I said, "do you take care of your girlfriends?" "Of course," he said.

So he became my new boyfriend number two; boyfriend number one was young, cute and broke. Well, I salivated when I thought about all the cookies, ice cream and other foods I could buy. I was alone in the world, with a small kid, and it was my first time away from home, and—drum roll—with my very own Section 8 apartment. We'd dine, dance and love. What a great boyfriend number two! There was food, and mo' food—my crack, my weed, in *food form*! My once-a-month welfare check only went so far! And the food stamps were used up the first week of the month.

Dropping out of college was not an option; it was how I was going to build my "empire" for me and my family! Cookie from the 2015 hit TV series "EMPIRE" did 17 years in jail, and Luscious sold drugs to get some traction establishing their business, I, on the other hand, financed my college years with part-time minimum-wage work ($2.10/hour), boyfriend number two, public transportation, monthly government checks, food stamps and a government apartment! My insides never lost track of two things: completing my college degree and my desire to act with morals! Even if I fell short of my ideals, it only lasted a short amount of time.

Part Three: Looking For Healthy Love

"The journey of a thousand miles begins with a single step."

Lao-tse

New Boyfriend

My romance goal was getting the best of me. My life consisted of college, part-time work, being a single mom and searching for a serious courtship. William Ringfield and I were on and off as much as a light switch. I needed a boyfriend to keep my sanity, as I was on the edge most days.

I met a cute guy named Dennis while waiting on the bus. I was headed to the hospital because I felt sick. He said, I'll go with you and he did. We waited at the hospital until I was seen by the doctor and given a prescription for a tummy virus. He and I caught the bus home and he asked if he could be my boyfriend. I said, Yes, quicker than a person changing lanes on the expressway. I was like a deflated balloon suddenly filled up with air. I had a reason to be happy again. He was a quiet guy but had no means of income. I didn't care as I had my own money that I kept for me. I had one criteria for my guy—you must have your own money or at least you weren't getting mines. I did know that much. He never gave me money nor did he ever ask for my money. He and I got along pretty well until that crash and burn day when he brought up another girl's name, "Breanna!"

Dennis initiated conversations about how Breanna needed a place to stay, and asked whether she could stay with me and him in my project apartment – a mild version of *Sister Wives*. The thought of Dennis not being with me caused Okay to come out of my mouth. This is the impact of poor parenting that plagued me. I felt deathly ill if I was alone.

I was so freaking needy that I craved a day-to-day companion…sadly, by any means necessary. Sure, Breanna can stay with us… "Just don't break up with me" echoed from my inner being. I can still hear it. The honor-roll college student was living in a government apartment, with her user boyfriend and his other girlfriend who turned tricks for him. Aren't I a piece of work? This went on for a while, and as you will see throughout my story, *a common theme: my son, later sons were the only thing that could penetrate or awaken my damaged consciousness*, so that I could clearly see my bullshit. And this living arrangement was bullshit in the third degree.

My son, Kornelius, now two years old, started imitating adult behaviors in his crib from Dennis and Breanna's conduct--- what the hell! I was horrified and flabbergasted! "What kind of role model am I for my son?" Within seconds, with eyebrows scrunched, I asked Dennis, Breanna, and their child to leave my welfare apartment and never return. Damn, hard to imagine, but they were sicker than I was! Children are to be protected by their parents. A third thing I couldn't shake was the mistreatment of children. Dang, just close your door; how hard is that. You gotta draw the line somewhere! They left for good. Homey, don't play dat!

I sat in my living room, and with slurred words, hugged and apologized to my two- year- old son for not taking into consideration how my choices could directly influence him.

FRED...WILL YOU MARRY ME?

Fast forward a few years. I had completed college and landed a teaching job! I was approaching 25 and full of despair about not being married because society gave you one singular message, "You are a misfit" if you are not married by then. Society, the world's opinion, had me in a cartoon-like state spooning out make believe rules as if one rule fits all. Instead of saying take your time to become whole and authentic, he will come along or not and either way you are perfectly Okay and enough.

Feeling public pressure similar to peer pressure I reflected upon the fact that every relationship had failed and failed miserably. I felt like a female tiger after a kill. Panting, walking to and fro, in deep thought about what was to be my next move...my prey...my husband, as society pressures you to think this is mandatory to be considered "normal." And I was a sucker for any glimpse of "normal."

I knew I craved the admiration that came with the victory of marriage. It would say to me and the world that, "I am somebody...finally." This damaged girl would be fixed, or so I mistakenly thought.

My relationship with my boyfriend, Fred was his name, the beautician was sinking like the Titanic. He realized that, "something was deeply wrong with this zombie-woman!" We slammed into the approaching iceberg due to my erroneous thinking. Since we were now an item, I decided it was time to get engaged, so I went out and purchased an engagement ring. Shoot, I'm 25 and my marriage clock is ticking.

Dusk was approaching, and I heard Fred's key turn in the door. The loudness of the unlocking of the door made me shiver with both delight and fright! Everything seemed to be moving in slow motion, like in the movies. I had the scene played out in my mind; Fred didn't have to worry about all the details of choosing a ring, deciding on where and how to propose. Shucks, I knew he'd be overjoyed that I had taken the initiative to do all that for him.

We had dinner, went to bed and retired for the night. Within minutes it seemed dawn glared through the window, and I thought, "It's now or never." I silently got up and prepared for work as a professional science teacher of middle grade students as I had been doing for the last three years.

Fred was still asleep. To minimize a disagreement, or a lengthy disappointment, and with 10 minutes left before leaving for work, I slipped the engagement ring on my finger, walked to his side of the bed and said, "Fred, look—what do you think? It's an engagement ring. Do you like it?" I did all of this without any prior discussion with him. It seemed Okay to me…but I can hear Dr. Phil saying, "What were you thinking?" Or better, "How's that working for yah?"

He looked at me in disbelief and said, "Bonita, what are you doing? We have not talked about this!" In that hour-long minute…flashbacks of the things I had done for him flashed through my mind like a deck of playing cards. I had co-signed for him to get a new Cadillac car in my name, I had snorted cocaine with him (and I don't like even like drugs—I like twenty bags of Oreos, Kit Kat bars, Butter Finger bars, 3 Musketeers bars, and the list goes on. Whew! Drugs…yuck!), I had chosen him as my one and only boyfriend, and I had cooked for him. Shit, I even left the dancing clubs with my friends, and went home with him, as he sometimes snatched me out of the clubs. I love to dance; I love music. All of this and you can't do this one doggone thing for me? OK, buddy.

Engulfed in anger, I shifted into vengeance mode—a step higher than revenge; Angry black woman…aw, hell. Watch out now. Shit, you'd remember this, motherfucker bastard ass! I got up, walked away from his side of the bed and exited the house. Needless to say, I didn't see much of Fred after that stunt from, *Desperate Non-Housewives*! LOL!!! All I did was give him a *tiny hint* that I wanted to get married, and I wasn't really into him anyway! He was a, "he'll do," an old-fashioned settling. What's so crazy about buying this ring? Men are so freaking stupid; talk about "a pot calling a kettle black." I returned the ring, and Fred continued to pay off his gray Cadillac, but the demise of the relationship was permanent.

Didn't he know I had a damn hidden agenda? I was on a mission to get married! I was 25 years old, and American culture dictates that if you are not married by 25, "You are an old maid," and I would be damned if I, Bonita, was going to fall into *that* stinking category. I was too young and inexperienced to tell humankind I'd rather be alone and happy, than sick with you…Thanks, Dr. Phil and Ms. Queen Oprah for those healthy words!

I regrouped and pulled out my natural God-given talent of resilience. I was a gifted bounce-back gal! As in *Rawhide*, an old cowboy TV series in the 1960s, slap, slap and get moving. *Rawhide-keep it moving-* was my philosophy for life; just keep moving, regardless of the setbacks and insane decisions, as I had made many.

My plan for snatching up a husband wasn't producing the desired results. I pulled out another natural trait: I love to think and analyze. After many days of thoughtful examination of my dealings in romantic relationships, I was raising my stakes. No hanky-panky before marriage.

Heck, up until now, sex was for the guy's sake. I didn't get a lot out of it. I always heard my grandmother's voice: "You have sex for them; they are the ones who have all the fun. You are just an emotionless participant." So, I was pulling the plug. I wasn't getting what I wanted, so you were not getting what *you* wanted---Pleasurable lovemaking, No!

    I felt really peaceful about my decision. My self-esteem soared. Finally, I was taking a step toward honoring myself, which was long overdue. Woman in the Mirror; make that change-Michael Jackson. YEAH!!! I went out on the town to an upscale dance club; while in revenge mode. A gentleman asked for my number. He called the next day, and I told him I was engaged (a big, super-duper lie). I just wasn't over Fred. We ended the phone call with him saying, "If, for any reason, it doesn't work out, keep my number, and give me a call." I agreed, returned the phone to the base, and did my "happy dance." A man thought enough of me to say that. Wow. I was in love already! And again, my esteem spiraled upward. I sizzled with joy, love and happiness…it will make you do wrong…it will make you do right; Al Green, of course!

EDWARD SENIOR III

Sometime later, emotionally better from my fantasized broken engagement to Fred, I picked up the thousand-pound phone and called him. His name was Edward H. Senior III. He wasn't home, so I left a message with his mom, who was in the beginning stages of Alzheimer's disease. I'm amazed she remembered to give Edward III my message. I resumed my activities for the day, and accepted my fate. No husband yet! But I also felt very good about my decision to be celibate. There was something so cool, so spiritual about this small act of religious obedience—it was a form of repentance.

    Deep in thought! Mulling over my days with mom Beulah and wanting to find a way out of the quicksand beneath my feet was no easy task.

Mom Beulah left her destructive mark on me, crippling me for a large portion of my early life. Why was she like that?

She always hung over me like a tornado slamming me in any direction it arbitrarily chose.

Ring, ring, ring, sounded my phone. On the other end was a male voice, saying, "Hello, this is Edward Senior III; my mom said you called."

"Yes, I did. This is Bonita. I called to say Hello and that it didn't work out with my last relationship." The conversation continued and we decided to go out the next day on a date.

We had a lovely date. He walked me to my apartment door. We kissed in peck style. He then left for home. Once inside my place, I shouted out, "Yes!" A shift had taken place—"self-correcting," I call it. It was *real*! Never again would I dishonor myself in a disguised plot to manipulate a guy into marriage. All I ever truly wanted was to do things the good way. I just didn't know how.

The nine years of dating nightmares were over. Meeting men in bars, at bus stops, on the street, at parties, in the public housing projects, and near misses to the neighborhood health clinic had all come to an end. The solution was simple: sexual abstinence! Even the famous Steve Harvey supports this decision with his suggestion of keeping the cookie in the cookie jar as seen in his movie and books until you know each other. God knew what He was saying all along: Wait. Somehow the involuntary impulse to sacrifice myself had loosened its magnetic grip. I felt freedom that night.

We had a few more dates, each one ending the same: with a medium peck-style kiss and a hug. With more confidence in his intentions, I allowed him to come in and sit in the living room as I finalized my getting ready for our date. I hadn't been in my apartment for long. No curtains were up yet, so I apologized to Eddie III, and told him that I had just recently moved in. He unexpectedly responded, "It doesn't matter; you won't be here for long!"

I smiled in disbelief and shock, but stayed quiet. I did not want to spoil the moment—the moment I'd been working for my whole adult life. This was my Cinderella moment. My prince had finally arrived. A triple wave of "WOW" shot through my being.

We never *jointly* talked about that statement again. However, he indirectly proposed after four dates and I was off to the races, planning our wedding. What Edward III did not know is that he could not imply a thing such as marriage, because I would take that ball and run with it—and that's just what I did.

I finally included him in the plans after I had, without his consent, set the date by calling the church. I did all of this without discussing it with him. My fear was so great that I was consciously blind to the fact of how unhealthy this was, and it appeared sensible to me.

Somewhere, in this single-minded plight to get married, I, at some point, *did* talk to him about the wedding. To my relief, he was reluctantly Okay with everything, as I had already started planning the big day. The planning for the wedding was in progress and he joined me with all the details. We then added overnight stays at my place, or his. We were in love and very happy. Three months from our first date, we were married. I was 26 and definitely not an "old maid." Did you hear *that*, tyrant civilization?

Planning the wedding was wonderful. I got busy with the details of my wedding. Eight groomsmen and eight bridesmaids were in it. My oldest brother, Danny, gave me away, since my alcoholic dad was deceased. My longing for family unity was evident, as I included as many brothers, sister and cousins as possible. Then I asked friends at work and my neighbors to join in. It was beautiful: my special day. On to the next goal: getting my master's degree. YEEK!!!

Oh, yeah! The wedding! Well, there was an attempt to spoil this fabulous day of mine. Mom Beulah participated in the wedding, but she was not happy for me, and it is evident in the wedding pictures. I blocked it out, as I did my whole life. What does a daughter want more than anything---*For her mother to be proud of her;* to say, "Job well done!" And in my case, additionally hearing her say, "I was wrong about you. I am sorry for thinking you would be nothing, for thinking you would be a failure and a zero. I'm sorry daughter; please forgive me."

To the contrary, she hunted like an eagle, searching for food from the sky, searching for something, anything, to spoil the day—"my day." We were at the reception celebrating and dancing, just having a good time. My new husband even sang to me the song "My Girl." "I got sunshine, on a cloudy day; when it's cold outside, I got the month of May. I guess you'd say, what can make me feel this way? My girl, my girl...Bonita. I'm talking bout my Girl" Awwe, awwe, awwe! Better than a fairy tale.

Well, mom Beulah, and her accomplice, my sister Debbie approached me and began in an "I told you so" demeanor, their "you can't be successful, you won't ever succeed at happiness" message, because "guess what I just saw." She began to tell me that my husband had just hugged a white girl, and that meant she is his girlfriend, just like on soap operas such as *General Hospital*, *Days of Our Lives*, and so forth. So he must be sleeping with her. "You need to do something about that right now. Go in there and end this marriage—now!" My sister Debbie was also saying, "Yeah, Nita, I saw it, too. He was hugging this white lady. Kick his ass and hers, right now."

I did my usual, unhealthy, childhood *coping* behavior. I smiled, I remained calm, stuffed my "at them" horrified emotions, and told them that Ed was in a spiritual recovery fellowship, and that they hug each other on a regular basis. That lady is Linda, and she attends their fellowship. Hugging is foreign to my mother, and so she just doesn't understand the existence of non-romantic hugging. To her, it was, "You are a damn liar Bonita. All hugging between women and men is sexual." Whew! It was Rod Sterling's *Twilight Zone*; a blend of reality and fiction.

Mom Beulah and Debbie stormed away, more pissed off than ever, as their plot to destroy one of the happiest days of my life had failed. Doom and hatred surrounded their beings, and as a result, they left the reception pretty soon after that. I, on the other hand, danced and partied with family and friends, well into the night.

Later on in that splendid evening, the limo drove us to our Atlanta Hilton Hotel honeymoon suite. Ah, the wedding and the honeymoon was *fantabulous*! Better than that, the groom showed up! Yahoo! I had a small fear that I'd be left at the altar. I had been conditioned to expect things to go wrong. My husband carried me over the threshold; we were so in love. We ate and looked out of our hotel window at the gorgeous city called "Atlanta," and I cried tears of joy. A phrase in *The Color Purple* describes it best: "I's married now! I's married now!" For weeks, he retold that story, "Bonita cried, she was really happy!"

The wedding was extravagant based upon my meek beginning. Eight bridesmaids and eight groomsmen in my beautiful childhood church, in which my grandmother (then deceased) and mother were members too! I was not surprised that brother Billie Rank didn't show up…he was supposed to be a groomsman. Again, meanest brother EVER; the only person as a no show on My Big Day!!! Lovely flowers adorned the church pews and altar along with decorative candles in golden six foot candle holders.

I entered slowly behind four flower children who dropped rosy red flower petals; my oldest brother Danny—on my shaky arm as my stand-in Dad. My Dad had been shot and killed years earlier over a $50.00 gambling debt. Family talk on my mom's side said my granddad died a similar way. His body was found beaten near a bridge that he had been thrown off of over a minimal street debt. His body was never identified and donated to Emory for research.

Here I was, now the third generation – getting married. My goal was to have a happy, sustainable marriage unlike mom and grandmom. I was 26 and full of big dreams. In my inexperienced mind, I was invincible!

Shortly, thereafter my July 31, 1982 wedding, school reopened. I enjoyed teaching science to sixth graders. My school was 97 percent Euro-American and percent African-American. Awkwardly, I was lucky if I had one African-American student in my classroom each year. In addition, I was the only African-American academic teacher of a core subject. There were two Special Needs teachers and two Physical Education coaches of color.

In 1984, my middle school was both a *State School of Excellence* and a *National School of Excellence*. That's the equivalent of winning the Super Bowl; the number one school in the nation. The school was also personally honored by Governor Joe Frank Harris and President Ronald Reagan. These were extraordinary honors yet I was unable to process the jubilant distinction due to the lack of anyone in my family being there for me to say, "Good Job, Bonita!" They were my worst critics surveying my life with the hope of zeroing in on mistakes and human flaws which are sure to happen.

My husband Edward H. Senior III was not any better. I was alone as usual with only my colleagues to high-five me when great things happened.

Work was great, home life was a wreck. After the wedding, we moved into my husband's home. It was in fair condition with a basement apartment. I later rented it out to bring in more income because Edward III did not have a real job; he hid behind the pretense that he was an insurance salesman. I, on the other hand, went to work daily. This contrast of gainfully employed and fake employed became problematic. I had a solid standard that both adults should be employed sharing the household expenses. I would not accept anything less. Therefore, disagreements were rampant, eventually leading to our first divorce. After a brief separation, Edward III promised to stay employed. With that assurance, we married for the second time. We loved each other but could not make our relationship work…which was a big issue. We dared to try.

I became pregnant during my second marriage to Eddie III. On July 28, 1985, my second son was born, Edward Senior V, nine years after his brother Kornelius Darnell Ringfield Senior. Edward H. Senior IV died at birth from his previous marriage.

Our family was good for about two years. Edward H. Senior III worked and brought home his portion of income. We leased a stylish newly renovated southern home. We filled it with quality furniture. In addition, we each had our own cars. My husband lease-purchased a new car for me so I would have extra reliable transportation for myself and our two sons. We could be compared to the "Brady Bunch" with our blended families. It wasn't long before his daughter Trisi Senior came to live with us. I really liked our house, French doors, lots of windows, and great modern kitchen appliances. I had it all: great job, new cars, marriage, sweet home, college graduate and three children. As good as it gets! I enjoyed seeing all three kids playing together. I did it! This is my family: Edward H. Senior III, son #1 Kornelius D. Ringfield Senior, son #2 Edward H. Senior V and daughter Trisi Senior. I was fulfilled and satisfied.

My husband and I continued to attend our healing meetings devised to help you clean up your life. I felt victorious! But then, we started to struggle with paying all the debt we had accumulated. Before long, marriage two was beginning to sound and feel like marriage one. Burdened with money problems, serious trouble started to brew in our marriage. He'd create a debt in my name and swear on the blood of Jesus that a sale from his insurance job would be more than enough to cover our extravagant over- the- top living expenses. Feeling obligated to our relationship and believing what he had promised, I agreed to let him partner with me in regards to our household expenses. Our finances quickly spiraled out of control.

His mom, a retired school nurse, over spoiled him. She had purchased his house and car. He could borrow money from her without any terms of repayment. To make things even more difficult, she was in the early stages of dementia. Within no time, her son, Edward H. Senior III, started depleting his mother Martha's financial accounts to keep up with our over spending and his under working. He knew *ALL* hell was going to break loose if I found out he didn't have his portion of the bills which he foolishly made.

This came to a halt when his aunt, his mother's sister, sued him in court and got full custody of her sister. This was the beginning of our collapse.

In retrospect, this guy I married was living off of my non-lucrative teaching salary and whatever he could swindle from his own mother. We both loved him and foolishly expected him to be honest and responsible…not a chance. A bird in a cat's mouth had a better chance than either of us!

Little did he know that I was in the early stages of breaking through the cracked pavement of my still festering childhood abuse and neglect pain. This was due to regularly attending Al-Anon 12-step recovery programs. I qualified to attend these meetings because he was in Alcoholics Anonymous (AA). Ahhhhhh… sooky…sooky now as the song goes. I was gaining clarity and restored self-worth by listening to healthier people, reading literature and of course, working through the glorious 12 steps. I had the *courage to change* rooted in the seat of my soul. I feel these healing ministries get a bad rap sometimes as they can literally resurrect your life of despair. I proudly acknowledge them. I have that right.

With this emerging self-worth, I began to stand up straight, look him in the eye and request that he bring home his one half of the finances or I would be driven to end this marriage.

Afraid of losing me, he tried to work but could not maintain a steady job. He bounced from one quick pyramid scheme scam to the next.

On the other hand, I got up, went to work, performed with a standard of excellence and at the end of every school year I was offered a new contract to return the following school year. God's goodness and mercy saw me through the damaging events of my personal life and somehow gave me the ability to focus at work and do exceptionally well.

Similar to my childhood, much was going on in that house at 280 Chestnut Street but like pure magic, it never spilled over into my performance at school. I remained a near straight "A" student in the Advanced Placement (AP) class in the 1960s!

To no avail, he had made more debt than we could pay. We were stripped of everything one thing at a time: house, furniture, cars, credit, savings and eventually my job! What a nose dive; our plane crashed on the runway blazed in fire and smoke!

Of course, I resented him because I knew how to live within a budget. I was not a materialistic person; many teachers are not that way. We are fulfilling our calling to serve and to guide the young, to show them positivity and love. True teachers receive wealth of the invisible kind: peace, satisfaction, purpose, faith, uncluttered hearts and unconditional service fulfillment.

I proudly admit that wisdom and support flooded in from the Al-Anon and OA (Overeaters Anonymous) fellowships. My cornerstone at that time was the principles embodied in all the spiritual groups: honesty, hope, faith, courage, integrity, humility, self-discipline, spiritual awareness, perseverance and service. I safely and matter-of-factly ended this marriage.

I had given him two chances. We married in 1982 and divorced, then re-married in 1984 and divorced again 1988! With sadness, I waved my white defeat flag as the song of surrender played on the bugle…Good bye and Good night…*a change was coming!*

The Marriage Journey

Marriage would prove to be a chaotic highway. I had reconciled with my husband for what seemed like the 100th time, with the same results. He would not consistently work. I was ready for a change. My empathetic landlord gave me some time to move out, as he had witnessed the laziness of my husband, who refused to carry his half of the financial load. Fierce and determined to rid my life of repeated devastations with unstable men at the conclusion of my ninth year as a teacher in May of 1988, I decided to take a gigantic leap of faith and step into the unknown. I summoned up the strength to permanently separate from my husband, resign from teaching to heal my emotions, isolate from my first family, and start over.

I had begun to self-check my thinking…I thought to myself, I think I want to pause – my self-made sabotage pattern- in order to evaluate my lifestyle choices, and surrender the idea that a "Mr. Right" will make my life work, because within no time, the contrary happened: my so-called, "Mr. Right," made my life a living wreck!

When we first met, my now ex-husband attended spirituality groups and as a result, I began attending spirituality groups as well. GAME CHANGER; I was exposed to a pathway that could heal my cracked places, and with that in mind, I gathered up the faith of a mustard seed and decided to put action into what I had been hearing and seeing from others in my spiritual family groups.

My best thinking had led me to bankruptcy court, a resignation from my nine year teaching career, a broken marriage, and two sons without a place to live. Therefore, it was a no brainer for me to pick up this no-cost blueprint for living given to me by my spiritual organizations, and put them to the test. It was as God said in Malachi 3:10, "Prove me now" – to me! I took the verse and used it for all the areas in my life. The rest is an incredible journey of success after success.

But back to my, "Mr. Right"…chuckle, chuckle…the final breakup. Here I was again, in the yard with my husband, Eddie Senior III, blue lights flashing from the police car. I had called them because he had gotten belligerent when I asked him for his portion of the money for the living expenses. My long-time high school friend: Pamela Hardy, was disgusted with me because I kept taking him back. Once again, I would get caught on the insane merry-go-round of makeup and breakup. Then came the time where I would get beyond irritated that he made no effort to bring home a paycheck, and I would ask him about it. He'd blow up, but the last time, he threatened to injure me. His abuse was escalating, and thank God I did have a boundary. Physical abuse was unacceptable.

My mom never physically abused me like that. When I got a whipping, I always knew she hit me a lot softer than my brothers, and especially so much softer than my brother Kenneth. She was extra brutal beating Kenneth for some hallucinating reason.

As hellacious as this all sounded, I had repeated this pattern with men like my now ex-husband, since I was 17, and now, at 32, I was ready for a change. I listened to my groups when they told me, "Don't date for six months." Focus on taking care of you and your spiritual growth." At that time, I had a front plate sign on my leased car that said, "God Said It, I Believe It, That Settles It." That was my daily motto; my daily philosophy.

I withdrew $10,000 from my Teacher Retirement account and along with my automatic summer pay of three more monthly checks I was good financially for a while. I made a decision to strike out on my own, like Rudolf the red-nosed reindeer, in the classic Christmas cartoon movie, *Rudolf The Red-Nosed Reindeer*. The line from the *Mary Tyler Moore Show* theme song fit perfectly to describe my mood. *"How will you make it on your own, this world is awfully big, girl this time you're all alone! You can have the town, why don't you take it."* I began to immediately search rental ads in the newspapers for a place to stay. I was very relieved to discover Extended Stay Lodges, which had everything included in Smyrna, Georgia, my new town. I was so happy to stumble upon such shelter arrangements. It meant the world to me to find these living quarters. It was just what I needed. Synchronicity is a well-developed law when you consult spirit first.

I had prayed long and hard for God to deliver me from the chaos I had unintentionally created. My husband would not work, unless it was a commission-only sales job. I resented paying the bills, while he may or may not have his portion of the money. I would break up with him a million times, only to find myself unable to stay away, and poof, like that, a hypnotic power would take me over, and I would be back with him all over again. And the cycle repeated itself several times.

This on/off dance went on for six long years, and by 1988, "I's married now" had lost its glitter, and all my material possessions were gone! Nonetheless I had me, group meetings and supportive friends. I had filed for bankruptcy, lost three homes, quit my career, my furniture and my car was taken by repossession! Bill collectors were harassing me from every angle. It was sink-or-swim time. So I made the decision to swim to safety.

Devastated, I filed for bankruptcy. What a fall! I recall going before the judge with my lawyer, sitting in the witness chair, thinking, "How in the hell did I get myself here?" I was on the edge of a nervous breakdown, near its crack, so ready to devour me. But as always, the image of my two sons, Kornelius and Edward, came forward to the front of my brain. I would say, as I had always said, they deserved more than what I had gotten as a child, and immediately, I would snap out of it, and return to the present, hearing the judge saying, "You have been granted bankruptcy in the state of Georgia." Relief: a clean slate; however, my credit privileges were gone for seven years.

Right before I made the decision to redirect my life in 1988. At an Adult Child of an Alcoholic (ACA) meeting, I stared at a tree, and seriously considered hanging myself, but then I chickened out. (One may call this a, "pity pot party.") The suicidal thoughts had begun when I filed for bankruptcy. It felt like the end to me. Thank goodness at this ACA meeting, supportive friends stayed with me, and talked me through—by the time I walked out of the meeting the suicidal thoughts had left; I never once mentioned what I was thinking. I guess they heard it in my voice as I shared my *walk of shame* predicament of filing for Chapter 11.

For seven years, I had to adjust to living without credit. It was even difficult to rent a decent apartment. Thus, the one-room efficiency of the Extended Stay Lodge Hotel was a beautiful blessing to me. The many heartbreaking events had taken a big toll on me. This was my lowest point ever in my adult life. And yet, at the same time, I felt peaceful. I had made a choice to fight. I had decided to be a victor, not a victim, with the help of my spiritual leader Bishop Dr. Barbara Lewis King's messages, various seminars and books, and my spiritual fellowship groups and friends.

I had no earthly idea that I had made a decision that would change the course of my life for the better for the rest of my life. Bishop T. D. Jakes often says, "Your worst mistake can be the best thing that ever happened to you." Wow, he is right. I have been on a slow, steady upward-bound path ever since. I spent a few months at the Extended Stay Lodge, a year in a two-family duplex, working odd jobs such as Krystal's, Arby's, waiting tables at Shoney's, The Baby Super Store, a cook at a local community college cafeteria, and a teacher at a private Christian school. And guess what "I was happy as a lark" as the classic soul group, The Chi-Lites lyrics go. I had to gradually rebuild my strength. I was emotionally blocked—unable to perform my professional job as a public school teacher. It is demanding to say the least. I needed that self-imposed sabbatical.

In October of 1989, 16 months (almost 500 days) after my leap of faith into the unknown, I was called for an interview for the position of a sixth grade science teacher and got the job that very day. I went to that interview on the bus as my car lease had been revoked. With no family to support me, I'd financed two lemon cars then went against credit convention: I returned them. I was in a mess. Nonetheless, I continued to fight and stand on principle. I had to teach myself many life lessons by trial and error that I didn't and should have gotten from my parents and extended family.

I was so grateful to be teaching again, I let myself enjoy my work. I received accolades, kudos, and promotion after promotion. In less than four years, I was offered a position of assistant principal. I declined the offer because I did not have peace around that position. I remained a teacher leader and Grade Level Coordinator.

Change is Possible

Starting over at the age of 32, with six years of simple, practical, spiritual steps and noticeable healing under my belt, I had grown tremendously. I'd stumbled face forward into a glimmer of light. Like gravity, this light nudged me to safety, though it was still a great distance away—about as far as our second-closest star, Alpha Centauri, 4.2 light-years away—still, my new direction proved to be anything short of magnificent.

Once I knew how, I hit the reset button for what would lead to a much improved life. In that moment, strength and determination surged in my mind, body and soul. I couldn't take another minute of running my life on my own self-will, relying on my thoughts and actions. It was clear to me, and fresh as spring water, that something was greatly damaged and intensely shattered in me. I trusted wholeheartedly what I had learned in my spiritual meetings, my "other church," as I called it.

One guideline made you step back, and assess "your part" in life events. This is the key to the process outlined in recovery groups. To put it gently, I was miseducated by my first family. It had zero to do with academic intelligence or me. The naked truth was staring me in the face. I recreated this nightmare in my adult life, because I did not receive healthy love and guidance as a child.

I had sneaking suspicions that it had a lot to do with the way I was raised, or, better said, the way I was *not* raised. The book, *The Drama of the Gifted Child*, by Alice Miller, contains a lucid explanation of the consequences of parental abuse, and I recommend it to those readers who want to learn more. She states, "The damage done to us during our childhood cannot be undone, since we cannot change anything in our past. We can repair ourselves and gain our lost integrity by choosing to look more closely at the knowledge that is stored inside our bodies and bringing that knowledge closer to our awareness." This is how we leave the cruel, invisible prison of childhood behind for good."

Back to my fall, in the summer of 1988, I made the decision to resign from my teaching career of nine years; the previous year, I had already lost my house, my car, my furniture, and my credit (Chapter 11 bankruptcy), and I had flirted with the thought of suicide. The only thing left to lose was my sanity.

Checking out mentally was not an option at that point in my life. I had two sons—aged 12 and two—and I'd be damned if their childhood was going to be anything like mine, submerged in darkness, day after day. I drew a line in the sand that blissful summer, and put on my garments of strength for their sake, more than mine.

Instinctively, I knew to resign from my teaching career in the summer of 1988. For the first time, I clearly saw a pattern with me: even though the pattern was a horrible, insane mess, I'd return to it for "fear of being alone," my first breakthrough flaw. This dent in my emotions was ruling my decisions. Intellect and talent are a beautiful thing, however, they don't override feelings and emotions.

With seven years of group therapy under my belt, I bit the bullet and *Did It My Way* (Frank Sinatra). I spent 16 months in the wilderness, in the valley; quit my career, and emerged a new creature. I stood alone with only my two sons. I was determined to solve this mystery of, "How do you navigate to the good life…the life of prosperity and abundance…where is it, this Land of Oz?" I wanted the land of milk and honey.

Follow the yellow brick road; follow the yellow brick road, and don't quit --- no matter what! This message silently beckoned to me --- and that is precisely what I did.

Looking back, it was the greatest decision of my life. I had to face the unknown, which was terrifying—and yet continuing with the known, the familiar way, was 100th times more frightening. My life, as I knew it, meant certain death, but choosing to change with the help of recovery groups and church gave me a sense of hope and strength!

To recap, I was 32, job*less*, home*less*, car*less*, and a mother of two sons. I had no support from my mom or five siblings…um…where do I start? With the money I had withdrawn from my retirement account, I began my plan of recovery. At age 27, in graduate school, I'd learned of the Maslow Hierarchy Chart of basic needs, and it flashed through my mind. Again, hope surged.

I thought, "all right, all right, seek shelter. It is the second level of the basic needs of living that Maslow mentions; physiological is first such as breathing etc; I handled that level by leaving Edward III as I was not gonna be breathing if I continued a relationship with him…he threatened to harm me during our last fight.

Yep, find living quarters for you and your children. Indeed, I can do that. I cut all ties with my family of origin—they just made fun of my fall, and my mistakes, not realizing that to *FAIL* is simply the **F**irst **A**ttempt **I**n **L**earning/**FAIL**. I felt fine about getting a room, but God stepped in, and I found a treasure — a place called Extended Stay Lodging, with a one-room home equivalent, fully equipped! Wow, wow, wow! I had all the basics for everyday living. Thanks God and Maslow…Parade!!!

Stress free living from Edward H. Senior III, being all snug in my Extended Stay Lodge suite, having $10,000 in my pocket, three monthly summer pay checks on the way, cutting ties with my dysfunctional family, gave me a sense of accomplishment and peace that I had never known. For once, I was taking care of Bonita. Stevie Wonder's lyrics played in my head, "For once in my life, I have someone who needs me, for once I can say this is mine, you can't take, someone I've needed for so long."

I popped my fingers, and put my swagger on, George Jefferson didn't have anything on me; we both were "movin on up — finally getting a piece of the pie!" My pie was peace and freedom. I took a sabbatical from life's pressures and just enjoyed my sons. We spent time talking, playing, going to the park, eating out, watching movies, and just plain old effortlessly breathing, with no "man" trauma. I finally heard what my third recovery group had said, "Take a six-month break from dating, men, and romance!" Get to know Bonita." Sure, sounds like a plan!" The bottom I had reached caught my attention, and I did just what had been suggested. There weren't any, "you have to," there were just lots of worthwhile suggestions by experienced members.

When you've been homeless, your very own space is pure bliss. A blink ago I was put out of my house, after which I went through a series of places: an apartment, living with a friend, and then living with another friend, and I felt like a gypsy — a nomad, roaming from place to place. Along with that, I was in and out with my then husband, up and down, turn around. The results were always the same with him: "I'm too cute to work. The women in my life always take care of me."

That was the wrong answer. My response was, "You will carry half of the load, or I am gone!" I may have been attracted to bums, but this lifestyle for me had to change. And then came a turnaround, my very own Efficiency Room. Oh yes, God. Thank You, Thank you, God!

Yahoo! This lodge did not require a credit check, they were well kept and nice rooms, the deposit was one week in advance, you could add cable and a phone and it had lovely running water and a modern kitchen area — much more than I had ever dreamt of after my *fall*.

My frailties were like an undercurrent of water flowing and rippling through every area of my life. Nonetheless, an invisible desire tugged me forward, and launched me from a bitter wilderness, painted with self-hate and victimization.

My final year with my husband had also proved to be a positive one, it pushed me from caterpillar/worm to butterfly; I began my metamorphosis—a lovely concept introduced to me by my spiritual teacher Bishop Dr. Barbara L. King. From that one decision sprang forth a new life of win-win processes. Nevertheless, changing my life was no easy process—it was simple, but darn well not easy.

In my mind I relived this sad situation as I searched high and low for a job, quite aware that my cash was slowly and meticulously dwindling away. I took any means of work that would add to my disappearing savings. In addition to jobs like Krystal's restaurant, Hardy's, the Baby Super Store, substitute parenting for the mental disable, I did door-to-door encyclopedia sales. I would return to my one-room, one-bed Extended Stay hotel room and collapse while my boys played and entertained themselves, eventually crawling into our bed and slept. Days I'm not the least bit proud of—but these days did exist as fact and not fiction. Those were my fertilizer days—growth is painstaking.

I spent my days with my sons, working, attending healing meetings, reading, and job hunting. One evening, Kornelius couldn't babysit Edward, so he dropped Edward off at his friend Dwayne's house. I stayed at work, went home, and picked up Edward from the neighbor's house that morning. Edward was unusually needy and irritable, although he was usually a happy, bubbly child. Then he told me that Dwayne had taken his penis out and started playing with it. He continued to tell me what had happened in detail.

I immediately called the police, and we filed charges of sexual abuse, but the family swiftly moved out of state before the court hearing could be scheduled. Edward received counseling for as long as recommended. I never left him with anyone again unless I was 100 percent sure they were good people.

It was eerie and strange how abuse could find its way to me and my family. I sometimes felt like I had a magnetic abusive satellite dish attached to my head. However, I was also fortunate. A really wonderful family of European heritage lived one house over and helped to watch Edward as I worked. They fell in my lap. Thank you, Lord.

I got into my binge-eating disorder when the pain was too much. With the same old resolve on this fresh day, my out-of-control compulsive overeating was going to meet its death. And as usual, by breakfast, I was gluttonous, stuffing my mouth with food garbage. Give me a cookie—any cookie, any kind of cookie—I need to feel better, I need to escape this hell I'm in. My failure voices would surface, and I'd feel terrorized and doomed. The pain was torturous; I thought I would die, bursting into a million pieces of flesh. The suffering of this compulsive overeating condition and life left me potato chip–thin emotionally, although mentally, I was strong as an ox because I was regularly attending group meetings. My mind was focused on turning things around, evident by all the gut level pitches in my groups; I called them private talk shows.

Fact wise, I knew that my state of affairs was caused by something greater than myself. I would always go back to a part of me that excelled without effort—the classroom—no matter how reckless my life choices were. I could make an "A" in the academic setting, while paying little-to-no attention; explain it one time and I captured it like a camera does a picture. The information was processed and stored rapidly into my mind, and in a flash, I came back salivating for more with hands held out. I had a deep hunger for information, facts and theories. I wanted this type of success with my home life. The search was on for the answer.

I took a break from men and dating to give myself a chance to thoroughly ponder the huge discrepancy between me and the academic world, as suggested by my spiritual group. I often wondered where all these insane incidents were coming from; why did they continually creep back into my life? It was enough to drive you mad, a lingering fear I wore like a garment for most of my life; "I'm actually mad, trying excessively hard not to be. Only a mad person would have come to such a fork in the road." My best efforts equaled an "F" on my report card—baffling.

I faced the ending of my career as a phenomenal teacher. I decided to resign from teaching because I could no longer live this double life. It was too exhausting. I wanted to give my full attention to getting better without the demands of my career. Further, losing my home and getting a divorce among other losses signaled to me that I needed a sabbatical from work in order to recover with dignity.

I was a Cum Laude college graduate who had outstanding credit, who was a former homeowner, a former new car owner, and who had been married to a drop-dead gorgeous guy in a grand style wedding; by sheer will, I had achieved all of these things, yet everything had crumbled before my eyes, like the walls of Jericho, with other people watching and snickering. How could all of my successes be erased by marrying an unstable man? My Lt. Columbo (1960s TV Show) thinking went into full effect, "This isn't adding up!"

Simple, I thought. I was mad, pretending to be well, sane, and all put together. Even though these thoughts were troubling, I had six years of spiritual recovery under my belt. At every "change your life meeting" I attended, I repeatedly heard that there was a power greater than myself that could restore me to sanity, and boy, oh boy, did I need to be restored to sanity. So I trusted what they said, and minute by minute, I plunged forward.

Weary with no major job offer, and before I returned to teaching, I got a life-changing call from my spiritual sponsor. "Bonita, have you found a job yet?" "No, I'm still searching. My Southern Bell job pursuit fell through." She then replied, "I can offer you a job at my college cafeteria for 250.00 a week." That was music to my ears. The few hours at Krystal's, Hardee's and the Baby Super Store were not nearly enough to keep me afloat. I was even turned down for public assistance, or welfare, and food stamps. My retirement savings were reduced to vapor fumes. I jumped at this chance for steady income.

At last, happy and relieved to have a job, I put my son Edward in an income-based daycare center and took my other son Kornelius to his eighth-grade class. My son Kornelius's school experiences were a revolving-door exercise; here this year, there the next year. I was totally oblivious to the emotional damage that has on a child. I was emotionally a child myself and I had children I was responsible for. Whoa!!!

My mentor said to me, "Bonita, I thought you were having a nervous breakdown, quitting your teaching career and deciding to work in the fast-food industry." Looking back on this period, this was precisely how I side-stepped a nervous breakdown. I had given myself a chance to rest, reflect, pause, and heal; a countercultural move, but well advised by counselors. I saturated myself with intuition and spiritual recovery. I knew instinctively not to add any job that required mental and emotional strength, as I had none left to give in that area; I was depleted and drained due to my divorce. I had only enough strength for rebuilding my life. Emotional work is the toughest thing a human being can do so I refused to be overloaded with a job that I could easily do later. My goal now is to rehabilitate myself. Without this break, I was doomed to repeat my life threatening pattern.

Further, I needed to find the authentic Bonita that I was at birth—the Bonita who existed before living with an untreated, brain diseased family of origin. I was profoundly affected by our generational illnesses and devastating deficiencies. Mental Illness, "the Silent Epidemic," as Bishop T. D. Jakes so clearly says!

With my sons in school and daycare, it was off to work I went. I was very grateful to my sponsor/life coach; I had no idea she was a manager, until that phone call she made, offering me a job. What an awesome example of synchronistic results at work, the late Dr. Wayne Dyer talked a lot about this spiritual force—which I'd come to experience more and more. This job at the local college cafeteria *only served to heighten* my belief in God.

Whew, I could breathe a little now; my sons and I would not be homeless, at least not that day. Some of my self-esteem was returning, and I'd been abstinent from men and dating for six months. Then I was told I could practice dating again. Eventually I met a guy. My sick neediness took over, and we were in an instant relationship, or so I thought. The discrepancy between what I'd intended, and what I'd gotten re-entered my life. In no time, I was pregnant, and he was in favor of an abortion. I'm scratching my head, thinking that this is the same old pattern, just with a different guy. I had the abortion and terminated the relationship, baffled by my inability to get this "man thing" repaired. This is where my dysfunction manifested itself the most—I was a relationship addict and a food addict. Damn!

I continued to attend my life meetings to continue my mental and emotional maturity. In line with that, I took another six-month break from men and dating. I continued these no-dating sabbaticals when needed, because I knew what I deserved. I just kept following the yellow brick road. I received hope each time as I saw myself clearly returning to functionality. Good guys were out there—I just needed to heal myself so I could enjoy their character and strength. You can't give what you don't have, for sure!

During all of this I moved to a two-bedroom duplex, red brick, with a fireplace. I applied for the place with bad credit, so I used my, "I was a teacher for nine years; you can call my former principal if you so desire." And my landlady did. She spoke to him, and he did verify that I had worked there for six years but added that he did not know my financial situation. Graciously, she decided to rent the duplex to me, regardless of my awful renter's history, my bankruptcy, and no-credit status. As Ms. Sophia stated in *The Color Purple*, "I saw you, Miss Celie, in that there store, and I knows der was a God." The next day, I was humbled and full of gratitude when my landlady placed the key to my very own duplex in my hands. I was overcome with joy and relief, that I had taken charge of my out-of-control, runaway freight train life by getting my very own territory!

I was bound and determined that my two sons would not experience the same childhood madness that I had endured, or at least I would die trying to prevent it from ruining their chances of normalcy.

Yep, so on to the next sane thing. I needed to get some beds for us. All of my furniture had been repossessed by the furniture company. I actually alerted them that I was *about* to file Chapter 11. A few days later I changed the statement I had given them and said that "I *was not* filing Chapter 11," not knowing that was why they had not come the first time to take their furniture back. No sooner than I had made that second call and statement, they sent a truck to reclaim their furniture. I felt so stupid; me and my big mouth!

In hindsight, I'm glad they took the furniture back. I was not able to pay for it, anyway; my ex-husband was the one who created all the bills. I was not stable enough to say to him, "No, I am not signing for this or that", I'd just put my signature on anything he laid on the table. Free from him now, I scouted out inexpensive, cash-only furniture stores, and bought some beds and bedroom furniture. Moving right along, I got a dining table and chairs. Slowly I decorated the duplex, and then I resumed my feverish job hunt.

Intuitively, I knew I had made the right decision in taking a year or more off from teaching, as I was emotionally exhausted and, had tender nerves that would not be able to endure the demands and rigor of a professional *Lead* classroom teacher. I had one nerve left, and that could break like a guitar string at any moment, if plucked.

The only jobs I was most suited for were the kind that did not require any emotional or mental abilities. I was down on my reserves—what little I did have was needed for the unknowns that life was sure to throw at me! The good news was that I was healing emotionally; I continued to attend support meetings. I was beginning to feel solid again, like my inside was packed with energy and substance, instead of being hollow, as before.

Part Four: Personal Growth

"Out of suffering have emerged the strongest souls; the most massive characters are seared with scars."

E.H. CHAPIN

Return to Teaching

My program of healing recommended a six-month abstinence from romantic relationships, and then after that, I was to get out there, and practice what I had learned about myself by dating. My growth would be revealed by participating in new relationships. I was getting to be somewhat of a scholar with these spiritual programs, as their way of life was beginning to reduce the gap between my academic talents, and my talent for making life choices, and life's natural consequences were showing some gains.

I was slowly changing for the better, and the cycle of abuse loosened its wrenching grip. The faceless dictator was so silently drove me to places of bottomless despair was gone. Glad to be feeling better, I focused my attention on my sons, for after all they were my greatest motivating factor for getting well. I wanted to give them a better life—not a life of pure *FRIGHT* like the one that I had popped into. I refused to let another generation walk in complete darkness, uh-uh.

A friendly white couple, who I mentioned before who lived next door to my duplex, took an interest in my sons. They would take them to Bible study every Wednesday. Somehow, they sensed I was doing my very best to bring my sons up right. I agreed, and they'd come by and pick them up, resulting in me getting a much-needed break. It was a good mental and emotional break. Less than a few months ago, I had turned my back on everything I knew, in hopes of a better life. I was beginning to see the daybreak in my nightmare.

These kind neighbors were helpful to me and my sons. They were the first people on the planet who desired to help me with Kornelius and Ed, without an agenda. They did this for us from their pure, Christian hearts. This spoke loudly to my soul. I thought, "There are good, kind, honest people out there, and this is who I want to be with." These are the caliber of people I wanted to be with all along, but my damaged psyche that looked like swiss cheese had drawn blanks with each attempt at "normalcy" that the attentive/thoughtful family showed. They felt like the family that helped me when I was lost at five! I could sense the serenity and genuine clarity.

Life was moving in the right direction. Being abstinent from men and controlling my binge eating disorder, I could get on with cleaning up the wreckage of my past. I gladly did what the God-focused program suggested, again, I was making straight "A's," but this time it was with meetings and programs. At last, my two worlds were becoming congruent, instead of total opposites. And yes, when I attended my first change group for my food addiction, there was a little pee running down my leg(one of Iyanla Vanzant Ideas), lol—really I was just scared and disturbed, I turned on the wrong side of the street, but gratefully no oncoming cars were approaching. I was scared, scared, and mo' scared.

I continued to look for a more suitable job while working in my program sponsor Barbara's college cafeteria. I went to the unemployment office often, and one particular day, a staff member found an opening at a private elementary school—Solid Rock Academy—a fifth-grade position was open. I applied right away, they interviewed me, and I was hired on the spot. I worked there until the summer, and at that time, there wasn't any work for teachers; basically, the job ended in June. No income for June through September? This was troublesome, but I managed.

Another hardship, my car lease ended and it had to be returned. They would not consider a purchase deal due to my lack of credit. Twice, I purchased cars that were lemons, as I was all alone, with no family, no significant other, no close friends, and I had very little experience with purchasing cars and with salesmen. I thought people were like me—honest. Let's not forget, I had to file bankruptcy (Chapter 11), so my credit was destroyed for close to seven years. What a strange world—no parental guidance or support. To top that off, I was saturated with deep trust issues—asking for help from my recovery family of Al-Anon never entered my mind. I kept them at a comfortable distance, in my outer circles.

Eventually, I did not have any transportation. The straight "A" student, the Cum Laude graduate, could add to her list of failures: no car. It was hurtful, yet I was at peace. I would reflect that I did not have to contend with my mother, who was still maddeningly toxic, I did not have to deal with my siblings, who delighted in my collapse. Best of all, I did not have to engage in poisonous insanity with my now separated husband. Plus, I was sober from food addiction and men. Not having a car was small in the grand scheme of things. Besides, Cobb County had implemented a bus system that year…I love those coincidences, don't you? So bus, here I come, happy and whistling as I ride. Freedom from my blood family, and acceptance by my family of love, made it all so worthwhile.

Wow! At this point there were only three days left on round 2 of my six-month break from relationships! Men, be on the lookout! I met a good-looking manager at Kmart. We began to date, things got serious, and off I went into a romantic relationship—or so I thought. As time went by, I noticed him constantly critiquing small things. His criticisms grew, and the romance went out the window. He was quite controlling in a bullying manner. I called it quits and resumed my round 3 of six months with no men. Again, I was gaining momentum with standing up for myself. No longer did I spend months or years in a dead-end relationship…What a feeling! Da-da-da-da!

After a year off from teaching, my strength was returning. I felt strong and ready to return to the profession I love—hands-on science with middle school students. I had a deep faith and a conviction that it was time, and that I would get rehired in the school systems.

I recall having a heated argument with my new and soon ex-boyfriend. He said to me, "Suppose you don't get hired," and I replied, "But I am." Call it intuition, or call it God nonverbally speaking to me. Somehow, I knew I was going to resume my career. I just needed to show up for the interviews and leave the rest to the universe.

Sure enough, I eventually got a call from Fulton County Public Schools. "Hi, Can you come in for an interview?" Ms. Huggins, the school secretary, asked. "Sure. When? 10 a.m. Monday." Joy rang through my being. Praise, thanksgiving, and strong hope gripped my thoughts. God, I need this job, I need this job. Father, Father, be with me.

This is the core component of all of my recovery work: to apply spirituality in all areas of my life. We do this by taking action, and surrendering the results. My action part was to go to the interview, and find out precisely where the school was located. Healing work simplifies the steps of a problem, or a decision. Thus, my focus was to arrive at this interview fully loaded and confident that God's Will be done, not mine. I proceeded forward. I thought to myself, "Hmm, I don't have a car," and this interview was close to 50 miles away in another county of Georgia.

I wondered, "What do I do?" Oh, oh, oh! Cobb County had just added a public transportation system…Yahoo! My answer was right in front of me; simply catch the bus. Mapping out my bus route took less than 30 minutes. Preplanning was a must, in order to pull this off. One miscalculation would prove a serious disaster. The synchronicity of events was crucial. Missing a bus could mean the difference between getting this job, or not. Sweat dripped from my brow like melting snow on a warm day. I was really nervous.

Without a steady salary for 16 months pierced deeply in me the value of a guaranteed income. I had now a holy reverence for my career in teaching. The many perks danced before my eyes—paid vacations, health benefits, great hours, every weekend off, helping children, and above all, giving my sons, Kornelius and Edward, a good lifestyle.

The alarm rang at 6:00 a.m. I sprung up, showered, and dressed for success. Kornelius got on the neighborhood school bus, and Edward was taken next door to the baby sitter. I kissed my sons good-bye and dashed out the door by 6:45 a.m. The first bus arrived, which transported me to downtown Atlanta. Next, the second bus arrived, and it whisked me to

College Park, Georgia. It was now 9:30-ish. I reached up and pulled the string to notify the bus driver to stop. I graciously got off the bus in front of Paul D. West Middle School. I made it! Hallelujah!

Quietly, I sat nervously in the front office, waiting to meet the principal, Mr. Michael Gray. Prayers filled my soul. I believed God would restore me to sanity and that this job would be the foundation for that restoration. As previously mentioned, on my last car I had a custom plate made that said, "God Said It, I Believe It, That Settles It!" That was my philosophy of life, even to this day—22 years later.

The interview, to my surprise, went exceptionally well. Prior to my demise, I accumulated nine years of incredible teaching success. However, at that time, my self-esteem was quite low. For as you see, my childhood trauma counterclaimed any recognition of genuine self-esteem. My barometer of my strengths was so far off, that for many years, I felt like an imposter to myself, and at any moment, others were going to figure that out, too! My esteem compass malfunctioned greatly.

Registering and accepting my own capabilities was unknown territory. My antennas were skewed in that department; a solid iron wall was erected, which no force could penetrate. Talents—"yikes, stop teasing me"—flashed in my head; as I couldn't absorb kudos at all. It had to be a mean joke. Mr. Gray read them off my application: "Cum Laude in college, 3.7 GPA, State School of Excellence, National School of Excellence, outstanding ratings by your prior principals…"

After a lengthy interview, Mr. Gray, the principal, said to me, "It's hard to believe someone as talented as you is still out there in October. I thoroughly reviewed the stacks of applications and was pleased to find yours among them. You have the job. Give me a few days to tie up the loose ends."

I could accept the job, but nothing else. It would take years to undo what mother Beulah and some of my siblings had done to me, it would be even more years before I could even view myself as adequate and able to stop feeling like an imposter. There were voices lurking inside my head saying, "If only they truly knew me, they'd be disgusted and appalled." I felt like I was a good actress, able to convince my colleagues that I was good at my job. I lived with the daily terror that they were going to discover my inadequacies and toss me out the school door, like they throw a low-down, dirty drunk cowboy out the saloon doors, and I'd land face down in the dirt and dust.

I got up early for this interview. I rode several buses to get there. Now that I had been in the school, and the employees knew what I looked like, it was no longer cool to catch the bus in front of the school. A cloud of embarrassment hovered over me. To save face, I walked one block to start my long two-hour bus ride home so no one could see me get on the bus. I returned home, praying and crying, "Please, Dear Lord…Let this job come through." I didn't want to count my chickens before they hatched. I was still afraid; I wanted my written contract to seal the deal. I'm better—so much better. Merciful God, I am on the right path now. I refused to live in misery, and I am willing to do whatever it takes to give my boys a shot at a healthy life.

Relief filled my world knowing I completed my job interview, yet I still had to fight my thought demons as I waited to hear back from Mr. Gray about a start date. It wasn't real until I was given a start date. Then, and only then, could I let out my long, 16 months sigh of relief. Ring, ring: "This is Ms. Huggins, secretary at Paul D. West Middle School. Would you be able to start Monday, at 7:45 a.m.?" "Is she kidding?" I thought. I replied, "Absolutely, and thank you very much." As Steve Harvey tells you, "Do it scared anyway." Fear was with me, but it no longer dictated my decisions or actions; my values and ethics did.

At this time, I was involved with three different courage programs. I wanted sanity like the night sky displays the moon. A phrase of mine that

I use in humor is, "I'm alive, I'm alive," from the *Frankenstein* movie. The monster was pasted back together from different dead people. Now the body parts had come alive, and I was ecstatic. I, too, was coming alive for the first time in my life—all of my parts were beginning to connect. I no longer felt shattered like pieces of broken glass. No longer did I feel cracked.

It was working. Seven years of spirituality-group treatment, and now 16 months since I had resigned to get to the root of my dysfunction had gone by fast—for it was October 1989 that I got the call to report to work at Paul D. West Middle School in East Point, Georgia.

It would be a rapid upward climb once I returned to being a science teacher of sixth graders. The one thing I adored about being in education was that it was a stable secure job. I quickly moved from Marietta, Georgia (Cobb County), to College Park, Georgia (Fulton County). I was back on track and better than ever. My soon-to-be ex-husband felt bad that he ruined my credit and sought out to get a car for me. To my delight, he did just that. It was a pre-owned Nissan Maxima, brown and beige at a "we finance" local lot. Living large, I thought never again will I take for granted a job, a place to stay, or a car. They were all wonderful gifts, not to be taken lightly.

A scene in the classic movie *It's A Wonderful Life* delivered by the main character, George Bailey, sums it up colorfully; He says, "Burt, my lip is bleeding," with a smile as big as the sun on his face. Other scenes in the movie; suddenly the stairwell's broken knob doesn't bother George anymore; he had an experience that helped him put things into focus, he finally realized that the greatest gift of all is life, family, friends, and love—not money or status, which are fleeting conditions. For sure, in a distant way, I knew I had all four, without even aiming to obtain them. I had life, friends, love, and a new, improved family: my spiritual groups. These gifts were a by-product of spirituality—a relationship with The Source, the Almighty.

Things were progressing well: my son Edward was chosen at the daycare center as the master of ceremonies, at age four, for their annual Christmas program. Earlier, he had been cast as the baby Jesus in the church Christmas play. Kornelius was in high school, passing his courses, and he would later receive a book scholarship and a certificate for being a hard-working average student—wow! Sprinkles of sanity were beginning to infiltrate my life.

My chaotic life began to show signs of consistency. The highs and lows began to even out. It felt marvelous. Throughout the day, I'd find myself smiling and blowing kisses in the air from the inside—happiness suddenly burst through. Esteem for myself dared to return in small doses. Finally, I had the capacity and criteria for choosing a man of substance, a man who more than matched my lifestyle and standards. The stronghold of my hellish childhood was diminishing, inch by inch.

My tendency to get involved with men like my ex-husband came to a screeching halt. Music lyrics formed in my ears: "Do a little dance, make a little love, get down tonight" (K.C. and the Sunshine Band). Scenes of Jackie Gleason popped in my mind saying his favorite phrase, "How sweet it is!" The changing of destructive relationship patterns took six long years—2,191.5 days, from 1982 to 1988—with no mother to guide me, no father to steer me in the right direction, and only guided by spiritual support groups, church, and my best friend, God (or The Divine)!

Many wonderful things fell into my lap as a result of being at Paul West Middle School. It all felt like it was happening within the blink of an eye. I now had caring teacher friends, and encouraging administrators (principals and, grade-level coordinators) show up in my work life. Looking back, this was the first set of highly educated professionals who mirrored back to me appreciation and approval of my work habits, as well as my on-the-job social behavior. Prior to Paul D West Middle School (PDWMS), I taught at predominately white schools, and the faculty did not offer much positive feedback or encouragement. In fact, several of them referred to me as the "N-word" teacher. Regardless of their bigotry, I knew I was good at my job.

For the first time ever in my life, I felt deserving of the many kind and supportive remarks made to me by my newfound co-workers and friends. Little did I know, this was just the tip of the iceberg. There were layers and layers of myself still buried beneath the ashes of my life on 280 Chestnut Street struggling to get out! The recovery journey just *CONTINUES*: trace it, face it, erase it then replace it. As I said before simple but not EASY!!!

Nonetheless, I had strong hope one day at a time. If I could press through my prior mess, then surely I could stick it out when the new skeletons woke up and demanded control and dominance and center-stage in my life, as they sooner or later did.

"Kornelius, Edward, wake up...time to wake up! I can't be late for work." We'd dash to the car, pop-tart in one hand, and cereal bar in the other. Boy, the routine could be overwhelming day-after-day, month after month, and year after year. By this time, Kornelius was 14, and Edward was four. I had been a single parent for 14 years, and boy, was I getting tired! But there is no rest for the weary.

I left work early and picked up the boys for a dental appointment. The sky was blue and sunny. I felt especially good, because I'd stepped up to the plate and made the dental appointment for each of us. Thinking enough of myself and my sons to go to the dentist for an exam and a cleaning was major healing work—major progress!

I exited on I-285 North, and I stayed in the far-right lane for safety and security. I was already quite uncomfortable on interstate highways. Moving past my fears, I reluctantly drove on them, only if the route deemed it necessary, as it did that day. An eighteen-wheeler tractor trailer was next to my lane, and I sped up to pass him, as I don't like being side-by-side with them. Too big, they spook me. As I passed the large eighteen-wheeler, it came into my lane and hit me from the left side rear by my back left tire, which put me in a forceful, uncontrollable spin. There was nothing I could do to stop the chain of reactions about to happen.

I went to the left, across three lanes of traffic on the expressway. The eighteen-wheeler went to the right, and came to a stop. At the same time, in a split second, I heard and obeyed a voice that said, "Let go of the steering wheel, and take your foot off the brake!" I did just that, and slammed into a median wall that stops you from going over into the approaching, opposite-facing traffic. Bam! Bam! A second car crashed into me when I came to a stop.

I thought, "I'm either dead or badly injured." My next thought was, "Are my sons all right? Dear God, are they Okay?" We'd just been side-swiped by an eighteen-wheeler, thrown across the interstate, and hit again as we sat still. It was nothing short of a miracle that all three of us were fine, minus a few cuts and bruises and the whiplash. I took the worst hit; my face was pretty bruised from slamming back and forth into the steering wheel. My muscles ached with fire for days on end. Needless to say, we didn't make our first dental appointment.

Damn, I thought. Things were just beginning to turn around for me, and now this atrocious setback. Being employed only a short while, I hadn't racked up any sick leave days. I feared being fired, so I took only a few recovery days and went back to work half- injured. What a miserable time for me. To make things *worst of worst,* the car was a totally lost; I had no insurance and I still owed payments on it. My problems seemed to multiply.

A teacher friend drove me to work. Her name was Wanda. I had anxiety/panic attacks if I drove myself. Now, the next area of growth would be a stable means of transportation. Mom Beulah loaned me her car, only to snatch it back before I could get on my feet. Her (undiagnosed) schizophrenic mind told her to stop helping me, since I wouldn't allow her to manipulate me into insane, toxic behavior. I had found a nice duplex home to live in, and it pissed her off. How dare I have a nicer home than she? In a jealous rage, she left me and my sons car*less* and displayed no remorse. This no car thing seemed to haunt me, Ugh!!!

Many details are lost in my memory about how I was able to get back and forth to work without a car. However, I do remember wanting a decent car because I was now gainfully employed with a secure job. Randy, my baby brother whom I ignored a lot before changing my damaged self, was doing well jobwise but like me his personal like was in shambles. Hmmm…how did that happened. He dated underage girls and was shot by the girl's relative. Fortunately, it was not fatal. Eventually he married an underage girl who enrolled at my place of employment as a seventh grader. I just prayed for us both…damaged goods. His minister allowed these child marriage practices with parental consent. All of this made the News in Atlanta in the 1990sand it was shut down.

Nevertheless, he worked as a security guard and had now purchased a home. I dared to ask him if he would co-sign on a car with me. I wanted a warranty which only came with large dealerships. One road-block, they required good credit or at least a co-signer. I pleaded my case to him--- that I was a low-risk person. I told him I was working two blocks away at the middle school and that I always pay my debts.

My current bankruptcy was caused by my soon-to-be ex-husband. Randy stopped me in my tracks, with a sinister look on his face, he said, "No" without an explanation because there wasn't one-- except, "I ain't gonna help you get a better car than me!" I hung my head and walked away in silence, not knowing how I was going to get transportation to my job. Envy, competition and hate ran deep in my family due to all the abuse. We didn't know how to come together to pull each other up. My brothers and sister and I were severely estranged, we didn't like each other at all.

I recall again this wonderful teacher friend who lived in my neighborhood gave me a ride to work, and I gathered up some money and bought a "lemon" car again. It was a "we finance" place, perfect for a needy, desperate human being such as myself. Shucks, my credit was ruined by my recent Chapter 11 bankruptcy—the result of marrying *twice* spoiled mama's boys (they didn't believe in the concept of a job!). Holy moly, will I ever shake the aftermath of being dipped in childhood abuse? It creates and leaves an insurmountable trail of tears.

Car Purchase 101

I entered the adult world with upbringing which contained no life skills—they were acquired through sheer will. Who walks on a used, "We Finance" car lot and expects the salesman to be honest? OK…only Bonita. Within two to three days, I was behind bars for driving a vehicle that had three violations: no insurance, no current emissions sticker, and no tag.

The car was towed away, and my sons were picked up by mother Beulah. I, on the other hand, was put in the back seat of a police car and swished off to jail. Mother Beulah got a kick out of it. She left me without the use of her car, and now I needed her to get me out of jail—all she had to do was support me by letting me use her car until I rebounded from the car accident with the eighteen-wheeler. Ah, lest we forget, this is mother Beulah we are discussing, who is determined to break you down to your least common denominator—she'll pounce on you, even after she has you down on the floor, with her foot on your neck. Her favorite threats were, "You'll need me before I'll need you!" and "When I die, I ain't leaving you a red cent!" I smell a tad bit of Joan Crawford's Mommy Dearest.

Once the paperwork was done, I was released from jail with a court date. I appeared in traffic court, explained the circumstances and was given an 18 month license suspension, of which the judge suspended--- outside the verbal punishment there were no consequences. GLORY!!! I voluntarily returned my third lemon car to the car lot. It was a piece of junk. Basically, I was being educated in an informal class of car purchase 101. I now knew to do my research and ask one of my four brothers to help me. By process of elimination, I asked Kenneth (brother number 2) to help me as well as to ask God to help me. I dared not to ask Billie

Rank as he wouldn't even acknowledge my existence on planet earth, my brother Danny had done the disappearance act since mom Beulah threatened to shoot him during an argument and brother Randy had already said he was not gonna help me. I still clung to my first family—it was all I knew—when I experienced a crisis until I changed and began to lean on my recovery *family of Love.*

After researching, I learned that Toyota, Honda, and Datsun (now Nissan) would give you reliable transportation. I vowed only to purchase one of those three. With my tax return of 1990, I took mother Beulah and Kenneth to a "We Finance" car lot. Big, daily prayers consumed my mouth and thoughts about this decision. After months of car trouble, I easily invited Divinity into the problem. I, without effort, received an image in my head of a white car with a black stripe on the side. I decided that, if I saw a similar car with those colors, I would take it home.

To my earthly delight, I did find the car that was etched in my mind: a Toyota Celica. It is now 22 years later, and I've never had car trouble again. I took home the white Toyota with a black stripe on each side, and it was one reliable car—what a blessing. I kept that car until it was time to advance—over eight years, and it was still running! I advanced to a gorgeous, silver Infiniti with leather seats and a sunroof. Next, to a Lexus 300, and today I've advanced to my first brand-new SUV—an Isuzu Axiom. Once I purchased the Toyota, I never experienced car concerns again. Hallelujah!

Just like with the destructive men issues, eventually with hard work, it was rooted out, and so was the transportation nightmare zapped into the nothingness, from which it came—a principle given to me by my minister, Bishop Barbara Lewis King.

The healing force in my life came from support programs. In this ministry, there are 12 sequential actions you can do to restore and rebuild yourself to your original condition before all the harm was done. Peeling the Bonita onion is key to erasing the damaging effects of other people. Who are other people to tell you who you are? Only you and the Supreme

Being of the universe know that answer, so I peeled and peeled, until my authentic, wonderful self was discovered again. All the mud others slung on me had to be washed away. It is a glorious unfoldment of self —pushing past the pain is *Epic* laced with bonuses! It was like a plant forcing its way through a tiny crack in the concrete reaching towards the sun full of vigor and life.

I See Progress!

Oops, I'm getting ahead of myself. Three years had passed since I had car issues, and I was dating a much improved quality of man. I had abstained from dating in six-month intervals countless times, as that's what the healing process suggested. In those no-dating phases, I grew by leaps and bounds. I got to know, love and respect myself, as well as to love and respect other people.

I was becoming more focused. I started to have more time and energy. I released the foolish junk, and it left a void. I recall it like it was yesterday. Kornelius graduated in May of 1993 from high school—suddenly, I had my total life back. I never dreamed I'd be left alone to raise two sons, but I had to just suck it up and get on with it; as a result, I now had a son who had just finished the mandatory 12 years of formal education. Yes, yes, yes! I repeat, he graduated in May of 1993, and in June 1993 I was in graduate school to start my fourth attempt at getting a master's degree in education. I lost all my course credits from the last three attempts, because too much time had lapsed. So be it—suck it up, and get on with it!

Life was becoming serene and doable. Show up and perform at work, get Edward to school, attend healing meetings, date in a healthy manner, and embrace the foreign concept of recreation with women friends. What a glorious place for me! The joy was indescribable. There was an absence of terror, no mother Beulah to say, "You are unlovable"; no brothers to say, "You are ugly, fat, bald-headed, and less than the other girls in your "A" class. I knew emotional freedom as I had never before; I swelled with joy and humble pride. I was becoming stable, confident, and secure. Freedom qualities that had been stripped from me as I wandered through the wilderness, living with five siblings, one mom, and one grandmother began to resurface!

So what others took for granted I cherished. I marveled at the day-to-day routine of life—what a present. With Kornelius graduating from high school time was given back to me to do something for myself: I could resume forgotten passions and hobbies. One of my greatest desires was to continue my studies at the graduate level.

Return to Graduate School

In 1979, my first year after finishing college, I enrolled and was accepted at Atlanta University, which later merged with Clark College and was renamed "Clark Atlanta University." But that attempt at graduate school came to a screeching end once a professor wrote on my paper, "Not graduate level." That comment pushed all of my insecurity demons to the front of my mind. The volume of each one increased—*fat, ugly, bald-headed, not good enough, condemned, worthless*—all screamed loudly at me.

Panic and suffocating fear parked themselves in my cells, and I instantly dropped out of graduate school. Criticism of any kind shattered my existence. I survived only by turning to my food addiction—shit, a bag of chocolate chip cookies, a vanilla milk shake, a bag of peanut M&M's, topped off with a Big Mac, super-large fries and a diet coke got me through anything. I would binge for a few days, and then, appalled at my weight again, I would fast and starve to lose that weight.

Humiliated by my grad school professor's comment, I changed my focus and decided to get a teaching job. After all, I had spent four years in college and graduated "Cum Laude" near the top of my class. It was now time to get employed, and grad school faded into the mist. I landed a job and was successfully employed at a middle school that became a state and national school of excellence, we were honored by the Governor and the President of the United States—teaching and being around children came easily to me. For some mystical reason, the classroom had always been a place of comfort for me—my bright spot in a deep, dark cave: my childhood home.

After teaching for four years, the strong desire to take another stab at graduate school resurfaced. Again, I enrolled, and was accepted at a new school—Georgia State University. I worked very, very hard at my coursework, and received two "Cs." And a "C" in graduate school is unacceptable. Frustrated, I asked to meet with my professors to dissect why I had received "Cs" in their coursework. They very kindly pointed out that I could not write in paragraph form.

Never before this time had I known there was a structure to writing. I thought you put a lot of sentences together, and that was it. So I thanked them and proceeded to ask for help from my language arts teacher friend at work, the non-prejudiced one. Like magic, wouldn't you know it? My best friend at work was Edna McGowen—a language arts teacher! I told her my heartbreak story, and she said, "Come to my house, and I'll teach you the ABCs of good writing—paragraphs must follow a specific format."

Again, my childhood, scattered brain caused me not to be able to focus—I could read, spell, and write sentences, but I lacked the skills to put sentences in an organized fashion called "paragraphs," "essay writing," and so forth.

This time, I didn't do a food binge as I had joined an organization, a "restore to sanity" program. Along the way, I had learned new life-coping strategies, such as asking for help, talk to your professors, look for a solution and work your backside off. It worked out well. After one tutoring session with my friend, the language arts teacher at my school, I got the few steps that I had been missing—paragraph writing, topic sentences, and then detailed sentences—all very simple steps but critical when writing a paper. Again, I swelled with pride—not "chesty" pride but the happy pride of, "I got it!"

It was now 1983, and just four years earlier I had allowed this to defeat me and send me into a food binge. However, this time, I faced it and took the necessary steps to overcome my writing failures, to see this work was *amazing grace*. How sweet the sound that saved a child like me—I once was lost, but now I'm found, going on to sweet victory.

Sweet, sweet, sweet—what a gigantic turnaround from "not graduate level" written on my paper, to two "Cs" on my second graduate school report card, to learning to write at the graduate level. So much of undergraduate was like high school—multiple choice tests, fill in the blank and very little writing with limited feedback on your writing. I do recall my College sending me to writing tutoring. But I just wasn't clear headed enough to get it. Now ready to grow, with this new information and practice, I developed decent writing abilities.

It was now June 1984. Feeling a little better about my skills at writing, I made my third attempt at graduate school and retook the two classes that I got "Cs" in at Georgia State University, and to my delight, I made two "Bs"—I requested another conference with my professors to ascertain why "Bs." The only time I ever got "Bs" in a course was by choice, because I was not willing to do all of the work necessary to get an "A."

My professor gave me high and wonderful remarks on my written papers (a vast difference from summer 1983). However, he said I did a fair job at my final exam, which was based on reading the textbook. Balancing reading and writing was still a stretch for me at that time. Subsequently, I accepted my newfound graduate school "B" and called it a truce.

The following year, 1984, I became pregnant with my second child. Needless to say, graduate school moved to the back burner once more. Eight years would pass before circumstances supported a return to graduate school. Kornelius was now 18 and finishing high school. With only one underage child to raise, the thought of returning to graduate school became fiercely dominant in my mind.

Afraid, having already made three "A-less" attempts put me on a hamster treadmill, spinning but ending up in the same place. An "A" seemed far out of reach—yet I craved an "A"; I'd always made "As", so what was wrong with me? Was I losing it, or had I already lost it. What was the deal here?

I had started to surround myself with talented people since the fall of the Bonita Empire in 1988. My current supervisor had this noticeable drive to pursue her goals. She told me she was in graduate school. I looked at her and said, "I tried three times—I just can't do it." With conviction in her voice, she (Principal Mrs. Lee-Willingham) said to me confidently, "Yes, you can, Bonita!" To this day, I love this lady. When I heard her words, I had a spiritual awakening—something woke up in me. Something changed—an "AHA" moment, as Oprah so sweetly put it.

The way I underestimated myself was the epitome of shame; I couldn't see what she easily saw in me. It's a hurtful thing when others know you better than you know yourself. At that moment, something quickened in me, something awakened; it was a powerful, spiritual moment. Mrs. Willingham was like God in skin, a "Yes, you can" statement from this super-achiever was worth a thousand cheers performed by a cheerleading squad. I was in awe of my supervisor's success, and her continual climb up the professional ladder, and here she was, telling me that I am more than capable of earning an advanced degree.

This was probably the first time in my life someone had said to me, "Yes, you can!" I had been told by multiple people in my family, "No, you can't!" I'd heard it so much that I had begun to believe it. But, thank you, God—I was beginning to reprogram my beliefs about myself through what I was learning in my programs of restoration. At this point, I was involved in three.

Her, "Yes, you can" resonated so smoothly with me that I found the shaky courage to enroll where my supervisor was getting her degree—West Georgia College (WGC). It was the summer of 1993, and 15 years of off and on graduate school had taken place. My arms shook with anxiety as I made the one-hour drive to class. My palms sweated, my throat was dry, and I was hyperventilating—Mr. Fear sat next to me, in my front passenger seat, and yet I drove on, praying aloud, "God is All There Is; Everything Else Is a Lie," an affirmative prayer from my New Thought Christianity Church, led by Bishop Dr. Barbara King.

Against all odds, I started my fourth attempt at graduate school at WGC. There sat this angel of a professor—she glanced at us with Agape love. Pleased to see all the other adult students, I found a desk and sat down, Seeing all of them made me think I wasn't crazy to desire to go to graduate school, and here was the proof—this class was filled with people that looked like me, in their thirties, forties, fifties, and beyond. A sigh of relief rolled from my mouth. Happiness stretched across my being. "I'm here! I'm here! I'm actually here!" like Whoopi Goldberg in *The Color Purple*, the moment she got her dad's inheritance of a house, land, and money. I shook my shoulders… doing the shimmee shoulder dance…sha sha sha sho sha sha sho.

Class started and this wonderful professor said something that stroked my shaky esteem. "If you are sitting here in this classroom, you have 'self-actualized.' According to Maslow's hierarchy of human needs, when one reaches the level of self-actualization, one has reached the highest level of human needs!" A full circle moment just five years earlier I was near the bottom of Maslow' tier pyramid. What a *HEALING!!! What a FEEELING!!!*

I was blown away. I had done (*wow*) my recovery work for the past 11 years and was now reaping the rewards. And the greatest reward of all was that, in the summer of 1993, I made my first graduate school "A". The bondage of abuse, poverty, alcoholism, and family silent mental illness was beginning to lose their power over my life, and instead, the power of spirituality was making its presence evident through the miraculous results manifesting in my life. From "not graduate material" in 1979 to "C" in 1983 to "B" in 1984, and finally "A" in 1993, over a 14 years span, with life in between, it showed clearly the result of hard work and faith. I love the new movement of 2017 called: STAY WOKE! Awareness and insight are game changers!

Transfer to Clark Atlanta University

A new confidence emitted from me—rays of "Betcha by golly, wow, this is what I was waiting for" song reverberated throughout my being. My first graduate school grade of an "A" was bestowed upon me. I felt as though I had been knighted by royalty. From that moment on, I was catapulted into a new dimension of living. The shackles of shame and inferiority lost their grip on me. I was never more myself than when reading, writing, and exchanging information. A concentrated beam of "yahoo!" shot through my being—I found my place at age 37, my niche in this world that summer, the summer of 1993. One month after Kornelius finished High School!!!

The scripture, Romans 8:19 sums it up best, "For the earnest expectation of the creature waiteth for the manifestation of the sons of God." Divinity is present---I found this *affirmative prayer* this morning (2017) as I edited once more this story, it is dated April 16, 1993; the year I resumed graduate school. How cool is that!

Summer faded, and signs of fall flirted with the morning air. I got into gear and prepared to return to work. I enjoyed being a science teacher of sixth graders whose disadvantaged home environments mirrored mine. Teaching and caring for each and every one of them gave me a genuine feeling of deep satisfaction. My students were no less than anyone else. How can they be blamed for being born into unpleasant and dangerous conditions? Each day my goal was to sprinkle tidbits of self-worth, for I knew from first-hand experience what lack of self-dignity can do to the soul of a child. Invisible emotional blood oozes outward and reveals itself in countless destructive ways, leaving its victim paralyzed and stuck.

Teachers saved my life by putting "As" on my schoolwork. It was the one good thing I had in my childhood, besides my grandmother. It took many, many years to believe I'd earned those grades and that I was worthy of them. So it was a pleasure to show up each morning for my students, and they felt it and reciprocated.

This school year was extra special. I planned on continuing my master's coursework at West Georgia College, now University (WGU). I wanted to take one class after work per semester. Doggone it, the inevitable happened, and my car became unreliable for long drives. So I was forced to choose a closer university that had multiple transportation avenues available. Plus, due to all my familial deficiencies, my GRE score fell below the acceptance mark. As with most of my life, I needed to be shown what to do, and then I could do it. The power of mentoring is life-changing.

The problem was that there wasn't anyone in my family who could mentor me, or tell me what to do. I was not going to let a score define me. That "A" at WGU kicked the door open—nothing, absolutely nothing was going to stop me from getting my master's degree. I was born to process information and share it with others. I was called to teach!

My son Kornelius had taken a turn for the worse after high school. He had little interest in college and began spending time with teenagers who made quick money. He stared me in the eye during a heated argument, and stated, "I'll never take as long as you to have money." Little did he know that quick money is dead money, or at best, a prison sentence. After some time, he received the latter.

I'm trying to juggle a career (in which I had received a promotion to Grade-Level Coordinator)/I was the sixth grade Lead Teacher Specialist, one adult son, a nine-year-old, a dating life, graduate school, and a recovery program. The pressures of life! Whew, Jesus!

The goodness of the healing program is that it keeps you focused, sane and healthy. I did my part as a single divorce mother, but I refused to *overdo* my part. We have a saying, "Give a person the dignity of their choices and allow the natural consequences to occur." And in the meantime practice self-care. Thus, after a nine-month gap due to car concerns, I applied for admission to Clark Atlanta University in the summer of 1994 and was admitted. This way, if my car needed repairs, I could possibly get a ride home. I took two classes every semester after work at night, and I graduated with a 3.7 GPA in October of 1996. I received a Master Degree in Educational Leadership. I made mostly "As" and a few "Bs" because I didn't want to work that hard in some of the courses and make myself ill. This is the same university that told me my work was not graduate level in 1979; tutoring paid high dividends.

During those classes, something peculiar started to happen. Many of my professors began to point out that I was an outstanding student, a student of distinction. At first, I did not believe them (still suffering from thin layers of medium self-worth). I felt like a fake, and I thought that at any moment, they would find out I was a nothing—exactly like my family of origin told me I was! It was the weirdest thing—even though I was unable to embrace their compliments, something was beginning to prickle through the ground as a baby plant does, breaking through soil. I was quite fragile, and my ultimate final goal was to get that master's degree—that's all I felt I was capable of doing.

Nevertheless, my professors were relentless with positive feedback. I was more like a graduate school "teacher's pet." I was encouraged over and over—yet my past kept saying to me, "You're a fake." My plan was to walk on egg shells, stay under the radar, and get my master's degree without any attention. Not a chance. As I entered my advisors' office for advisement about class selections to begin my master's, he looked up at me from his desk and said, "You qualify for the doctorate degree program." My eyes rolled to the back of my head, and I was unresponsive. Never in my wildest dreams did I think my GRE scores, or I qualified for a doctoral program. Stop playing with me…please…this isn't funny, Sir, Madam.

Clark Atlanta University, a University of Excellence- being a private university and a historically black college/university, had a different formula for calculating your GRE score—they add all three categories, instead of just two. It takes into account the bias of mainstream culture dominance in development of higher education entrance exams. This was a mere accident to me, as I had no earthly idea this procedure existed. It fell into my lap. Another obstacle vanishes into thin air—that was another spiritual moment for me. Um…God, I see you! The crooked path was made smooth by no means of mine.

Sadly, things were no better with my family. Mother Beulah teamed up with sister Debbie, and things spiraled out of control. She would go against me and say I was jealous of her relationship with my son, as I attempted to allow my adult son to reap the consequences of his immature, fatherless choices! I couldn't get through her brain that he was hanging with street kids doing the unthinkable.

Under the influence of not-yet-diagnosed schizophrenia, mom Beulah's mental illusions swung in her head as reality. Thoughts raced through her think tank, grounded in a downcast spiral of inherited sickness. She thought, "Bonita is deserting Kornelius in his time of darkness. I'm going to step in."

"Step in" was more like "take over," and that is precisely what she did. The rescue circle went into full swing. Kornelius would get sent to jail, and mom Beulah would get him out of jail, like a revolving door. Jail, release, jail, release…until the damage became as solid as concrete pavement! He was sentenced to 10 years in 1995 for narcotic possession, and distributing illegal substances.

Meanwhile, I stayed with my program of healing, attending support groups, and getting knee-deep with safe individuals. I continued to excel at my career as a teacher leader of science, giving love and support to my teachers and students. Being in recovery now for 13 years equipped me with incredible life skills, one of which was to stop scattering my energy all over the place, and I became beam-like focused. I concentrated on graduate school after work, and during my summer vacations, which became the highlight of my life. Just sitting in the classroom with like-minded adults and professors recharged me, like a battery recharges a cell phone. My insides lit up like a shooting star.

If ever there were such a thing as destiny, this was it, even though fear rippled through my body, which came from old neglect and poverty. Yet somewhere out there, in the vacuum of space, I sensed I was on my path of life, however shaky my confidence.

My life was bursting through like a ray of sunshine after an overcast, cloudy day. Oh my God, I, with over 40 years of life, grabbing my foot and shoving it in front of the other foot, could see my personal growth. The poem by Langston Hughes "I, Too, Am America" was birthed into my consciousness; I, too, am capable, loveable, talented, and a worthwhile human being, even though I was said to be defective by my family of blood. I was living the American Dream despite the fact that, it was a daily struggle to believe this about myself, but practice makes perfect. It began to stick, crumb by crumb, with all the good people in my life: professors, colleagues, and friends in my 12-step meetings.

One awesome thing about people who choose to put themselves in a repair shop is that they tell you to, "Fake it till you make it!" I did a lot of faking—my insides would tremble constantly, and the weight caused me to feel like caving in at times, but my inner navigation system (INS) stood strong and steady, relentlessly nudging me back to the task of following my dreams at the seat of my soul.

My dream was to receive my MA of education. I thirsted for it, and nothing would quench that thirst, except the completion of this degree. It seemed far-fetched, no one in my family even knew about an MA degree. They sort of understood a BS, but anything beyond that was foreign. I felt utterly alone whenever I thought of them. I resented being so different from the people who I loved and hated. There was a disconnect as vast as space, the final frontier and vast is an understatement.

I continued to trudge the graduate school mountain after blessedly receiving my MA degree, strongly encouraged by a team of professors in my department of Educational Leadership. Again, I couldn't shake my INS—I would veer off to the left then veer off to the right, and then I would stand still, or distract myself with things that were familiar and comfortable to me. My self-confidence waivered intensely! I cried out to God, "If I am supposed to pursue this doctorate degree (and by this time all of my professors had encouraged me to do this without me asking), please send me a clear sign as I am so afraid of failure and my insides shook from terror; the terror of being humiliated in front of my peers and professors, the same way I was humiliated as a child by my mom, some of my siblings, peers and some teachers.

As Dr. Phil often tells us, "It takes a 1000 praises to erase the damage of one criticism." Growing up in my home, I was for sure criticized and put down daily and sometimes several times a day. My talk to God was, "You expect this cracked person, Bonita, to stand up and say to the world, 'my new goal is to attain an Ed. D.' God, you have got to be kidding me. I'm so happy with my MA—that's miracle enough for me."

I felt like Moses when God asked him to return to Egypt to free the Israelites—fragile, ill-equipped to do the job. Why me, oh Lord! May I please shrink beneath the radar? Choose someone else. I am afraid, Lord. The torment of indecision battled in my being. Not doing it felt worse than saying, "Okay, I'll give it a go." Thy will, not mine, be done. No sooner than I surrendered to this invisible pulling than I experienced release. My dissertation topic—discipline and the teaching of character traits/values — flooded my brain as I slept one night. I woke up convinced that God and I would do this thing together. Similarly, God parted the Red Sea to help Moses free his people from being enslaved, and this same God softly and sweetly said, "I am with you; trust Me, even if defeat seems so sure." And I tell you, I did feel that defeat would be my future prize. "Bonita, you are our first place winner of defeat. Congratulations!" Ha-ha ha-ha...psyche, a 1990s slang for 'fooled yah!'

You know, this back-and-forth war went on for seven excruciating years. It was a two-step waltz—progress, setback, progress, setback, progress, and setback! Quitting the program altogether happened in December of 2000, three years in. Exhausted, I just couldn't do another class, read another chapter, take another test, or write another paper. I had done three years of classes and tests for my master's, and three years of classes and tests for my doctoral degree. I was "book" and "class" and "test" dead. Energy for that type of life plummeted. It had run its course.

One year earlier, my brother Kenneth had died. I had not experienced the departure of a sibling before. His unexpected death, complications at work, and my first attempt at writing a doctoral study was a failure. I caved in! My siblings and I couldn't find sustained happiness no matter how hard we tried. Kenneth was the first to completely give up.

Brother Kenneth's Way Out

Growing up, Kenneth, brother number two, was always made fun of. I blew it off as everyday children mess; kids just full of "hater-ade." Without warning, he became known as "Monster Gay," and surprisingly, he embraced the newfound name like a champion prizefighter, who had just won the world championship. Not once did he express a dislike for it.

Even though my mom treated me unusually bad, the way she treated Kenneth was far more sinister. She nicknamed him "Bird," to say he had no brains—only a bird-sized brain, small, incapable of functioning normally, like a human being. Again, he never complained about it, or told her to stop calling him "Bird Brain"—what a kind soul he could be at times! It may also be that he was terrified to call her on it; Monster Gay in Public and Bird Brain at Home.

When he got in trouble, and got beaten with those electrical extension cords, Mom would give him an extra beating. You could feel the force of her swing on his flesh. Kenneth would beg for mercy, and she'd just hit him harder. Soon after that, we'd all hear him plead and say, "You're killing me, Mama, please stop—you're killing me! Oh my God, please stop!" And of course she didn't, and she swung harder, with a cynical look in her eyes.

I just completely blocked out my emotionally frozen terror. I was fearful that I'd be next. Once she reached that rampage level, anything could break loose.

This scene was played over and over throughout my childhood. You feared for your life on a daily basis. My mom was a big freaking bully—she dared any of us to make mistakes or to show feelings or disappointment. She reigned…mom Beulah was going to be the only dominant force in her house. Violence was first nature to her: she would pick up anything—broom, mop, shoe, tree limbs, belt, extension cords—and beat you down.

Kenneth did the best he could. He was born emotionally and mentally challenged; he was a tad slow. My grandmother used to tell all of us to be gentle with him. It wasn't until years later that we understood what she meant.

Kenneth struggled in school, eventually dropping out. He returned a few years later and received his high school diploma. Then he entered the Air Force where he stayed for two years, upon his discharge he received a honorable discharge. He had a hard time accepting his disability as well, even though his life was giving him some gigantic hints. Again and again, people took advantage of him. With a string of defeats in his life's tapestry, he finally, accepted that he couldn't make it out there in life and moved back home with mother Beulah. Big mistake—big, big, tragic mistake! Within a few years he would be dead.

Kenneth spent the last years of his life living with mom Beulah who was extremely abusive (she called him bird) but on the other hand she had smarts. She worked for herself by owning a hair salon and owning houses that she turned into rooms-for-rent businesses.

He worked at the Centers for Disease Control and Prevention as a janitor, and also helped her with her "room-for-rent" business. I heard bits and pieces of problems he was having through my other siblings. Without a thought, I did my usual thing of, "Oh, it ain't that bad."

When you have lived through severe abuse your whole childhood, you become numb to its deathly madness and consequences. None of us had a name, or a label for what we were put through and even as adults still subjected to. It was a ball of confusion. My God, my God, life was beginning to take a toll on dearest Kenneth.

Over the years, I had heard many sad things about Kenneth's affairs: every car he bought ended up totaled, every place he stayed ended up robbed and vandalized, and every woman he knew, used him. He once had a well-attended disco business, but it lasted only one day—his employees (mostly our brother Billie Rank's in-laws and friends) robbed him the first night.

Strange when I think about it, Billie Rank had a thriving disco business at the time and based on what I know about him, he hated competition of any sorts and if you did well, be ready to be bullied. He had to be the only successful person in the *Gay* family. It was like the Tale of the two brothers, in 'The Lion King'---Mufasa and Scar, Scar was willing to kill to remove a threat. Just recently, he said this about our youngest brother Randy, "he barely made it," and I wanted to vomit…there it goes again---the family illness. Whew!

Kenneth, also had a plethora of additional concerns, he was overweight and had a skin condition, a number of health issues, and a mother who called him "Bird Brain" on a regular basis, with a smirk on her face.

Is it any wonder, that around the age of forty-seven he began to break... to crack? As weird as my family was, we drew a line in the sand against crime. There was family talk that Kenneth had taken a gun to work when he had an argument with his supervisor because he didn't get promoted to painter, from his position as janitor at the CDC. He was fired, not exactly sure why, and was left with no job and no car. And don't forget that he was still living with ma Beulah.

Beulah's abuse intensified when he lost his job. She was meaner than ever. He was having a hard time and couldn't do anything right. However, luck was in his favor—he got a settlement from his attorney for an injury caused by a neighbor's German shepherd's attack.

Mom's usual thing was to take most, or all, of your money. Kenneth stood up for himself by refusing to hand over his settlement, so mean-spirited mom Beulah reared up the vengeance. She cursed him on a daily basis, cut off any interaction, and locked him out of his downstairs apartment. His break went to a snap...his cracks widened.

The madness against him escalated. Mom Beulah's last resort was to break her silence about Kenneth's behavior, telling us, his siblings, about his state of mind. I spoke with Kenneth, and he began to tell me that the Atlanta Police Department was after him, and wanted to frame him for murder. After many visits and talks with him, it became crystal clear that he was suffering from paranoid, delusional hallucinations, a diagnosis my sister Debbie had received when I sought an in-home visit by a county mental-health worker. He was not in possession of a sound mind.

Kenneth, after what seemed to be a lifetime of heartbreak, had crossed the line into insanity. Every solution I tried to help him backfired. So I called Danny, Billie Rank, Debbie, and Randy to try, one more time, to see if any of them could get him to snap out of it—but to no avail. I enlisted the help of the Georgia Department of Behavioral Health and Developmental Disabilities.

They came out and talked with Kenneth and concluded that he was a victim of paranoid delusion, and if two of us would sign him up, they would, indeed, do inpatient treatment. Of course, just like with Debbie, I couldn't get another family member to be that second person—they were all in denial. Who knows? It could have saved her. And it could have saved him!

Debbie left the family permanently in 2006, and none of us have heard from her since. We do know she is receiving a disability check for her schizophrenic condition. Her history is to travel from state to state, and not take her medication. I tried to save Kenneth and Debbie but there must be some level of willingness from the person in pain to consider help. It cannot be forced.

Even though no one in the family agreed to get county treatment for Kenneth or Debbie except me, mom Beulah continued to called me every day, saying, "Kenneth is acting crazy(new science data has learned it's actually a brain injury). We are so in the Stone Age when it comes to mental illness. Mom Beulah reported to me, "He's running around outside the house throughout the night. He's hiding in the bushes, and talking to himself. He's yelling out loud that he didn't murder anybody. He's fighting with policemen who are not there."

Nothing was working, and things were getting to a crucial point. And throughout this whole thing, mom Beulah wasn't showing one ounce of empathy for Kenneth. She was more concerned with what the neighbors would think and what the mental-health staff would think if they went downstairs and saw the condition of the basement he was living in. "Filthy" didn't come close to describing his dwellings…they were actually deplorable. A few weeks later she nailed the basement shut to block others form viewing it!

As for me, I was trying to handle all of the family curses, in between graduate-school semesters where I was taking doctoral classes, a full time mom and teacher. While Kenneth was going through this crisis, I was between the summer and fall semesters. The school year was also close to opening. I had a full-time career as a lead teacher. How could this be? Wake me from this lingering nightmare. Wake me, please! Why is it that my family experience was filled with so much cutting pain? There must be an answer—and there was, but I did not get it until ten years later.

Kenneth was half normal, half mad, but where did it come from? How could this be? What was its origin? There must be an explanation, I thought. But there was no time to ponder that. Our solution—rather mom Beulah's solution—was to take Kenneth to Grady's inpatient Mental Health Facility wing, the notorious eighth floor.

We loaded up two cars; Debbie, Billie Rank, and I asked Kenneth to join us. After much prodding, he reluctantly got in, and we drove to Grady Memorial Hospital, parked, and went to the in-patient ward. This is the department where the death switch was set off. County hospital policy requires that a new patient be evaluated first in the in-patient wing, Grady's eighth floor and then the doctors would recommend outpatient services, if warranted.

Kenneth, acting from his normal side, hesitated first but then reluctantly agreed to walk to the in-patient wing. Without warning, he hesitated again as we walked through the first-floor hospital doors. He had the expression of, "I'm not sure about this" written all over his face but cooperated anyway.

Our mother was nowhere in sight—she told us back at the house that she would join us there a little later. Bull crap...she needed to come with us from the start; not later! She had no interest in accompanying her ill son to the hospital with his three siblings—one brother, two sisters. Cynical, I tell you... Cynical. He wanted his mother's love and approval, as all kids do. God, help us, please! Where is mom Beulah?

Nonetheless, we continued our mission. Security checked us in. We rode the elevator to the eighth floor, got off, and then walked to the mental-health entrance. All of a sudden, Kenneth refused to walk through the entrance. We all began to attempt to persuade him to make those final few steps toward his comeback, because we knew that here, he would get the treatment he needed. American spiritual teacher and author Iyanla Vanzant says, "When you face your greatest fears and trudge forward anyway, SCARED almost paralyzes you," again as she says "a little pee may trickle down your leg." An exaggeration but you get the point. In other words, the fear is overwhelming and very very much real! We longed for our familiar Kenneth to come back—the one who did his personal best to make his life work.

Persuasion did not work this time. "I agreed to outpatient services," he retorted. Outpatient! Getting him to see that you needed an inpatient psychiatric evaluation before receiving outpatient services got lost in the confusion, and his abnormal half came alive. With three siblings saying he needed services, a staff nurse said the final tragic words to Kenneth: "Sir, you are not leaving here today." He yelled the usual, "I want outpatient services only," and within seconds, he pulled out a gun and pointed it at them. He backed away and then jumped on the elevator.

We all scattered like roaches when the light is turned on. I remained on the floor, ran for cover in the nearest bathroom, and locked the door. I refused to die like this, in a mental-health dispute. Images of my two sons flashed through my mind—I concluded they deserved their mom.

I knew from first-hand experience the power of the mother role in the lives of their children; how it can leave an unfillable hole that only spirituality can fill. I remained in that locked bathroom until I felt ready to resume this crisis, which was about ten minutes later.

As he got off the elevator, with his pistol in his hand, he tried to run for home. He was shot and killed on the spot, by an off-duty police officer, who was also working as an armed hospital security guard. His delusional fears had come true. My lifelong nightmare just spiraled into a living Hell too devastating to bear.

While I didn't witness the shooting, as I had protected myself from the violent scene by closing myself off in the bathroom, I felt as if I did, because I saw him pull out the gun and wave it around as he dared anyone to hold him there against his will.

Kenneth lost his battle with mental illness and died that day. I wept uncontrollably and had to be driven home by my sister-in-law, Judy. There was a common divine theme throughout my journey—a sistah friend would show up on the scenes when I was at my lowest…she hugged and walked with me as I screamed out my pain on the hospital floor. Thank you sistah-in-law Judy—my angel, my hero that day my brother died. My family of origin was incapable of showing feelings of love or support… what a tragedy!

Being yelled and screamed at were commonplace in my childhood home. Living there was a wide awake nightmare of monumental power. As an adult, I had puzzling panic attacks, flashbacks of self-inflicted violence, and layers upon layers of fear. Therapist number five called it a "curse"; sick behavior passed down from generation to generation. Just as we can pass on cancer or diabetes genes, families can pass on external diseases. It's like being injected with thinking and behavioral poison—slowly killing our lives. I have two deceased brothers and possibly one deceased sister—her whereabouts have been unknown now for more than seven years—that validates the fact that we kids experienced madness at the hands of our caretaker.

Thank goodness I was finally diagnosed with- Post Traumatic Stress Disorder, aka PTSD, which is treatable with medication or prayer; I chose the latter, with the help of a Christian-based therapist. For sure, without a plan of action, I would have continued the cycle of self- destruction. Having a clinical name for this was healing as well as soothing—otherwise, you'd think you were losing your mind. As Dr. Smith would say in a classic TV series, *Lost in Space*, "The pain, the pain, the pain!"

Doctoral Push

Losing my first sibling to suicide by police while pursuing my Doctor of Education degree ripped my heart out; I could barely function. I could not fathom the depth of darkness one must reach to actually kill themselves…that continually gnawed at me. I was stuck at the ten-yard line, things were looking pretty impossible. Yet the end zone was only ten yards away. I could see it, smell it, feel it, as well as taste it. Nonetheless, real obstacles stood in my way: after a two-day, ten-hour comprehensive exam, I learned that I had failed the graduate statistical section--- I got as far as tenth grade geometry; then I took other courses. Some months earlier, I had failed the department writing exam, which I retook and after some tutoring, eventually passed.

A few months later, the first three chapters of my dissertation were rejected by my department, as well as by a close and trustworthy friend. It felt like vultures were circling overhead, ready to strike my failures as if they were road kill! I quit!" "Throw ya hands in da airrr, like you just don't carrrrre" as the song goes—that was me.

I decided to be very happy and grateful with my Specialist Degree (Ed. S.) which you automatically receive as you worked towards your doctorate after completing your Ed D. coursework, even this accomplishment was beyond my wildest dreams. But wouldn't you know it, spirituality does not function in "standing still." It demands continual growth, continual evolvement, whether you want it or not. I love it when Oprah says, "God, don't teach me anything else today!"

Wouldn't you know it, a month or two later, somehow a new hire, Dr. West came to teach at my middle school. As a new faculty member, she was asked to introduce herself. During her introduction, she mentioned the thrill of finally completing her doctoral program. I truly admired her, as I knew first-hand all that goes into that endeavor. Inexplicably, we were drawn to each other. Eventually I shared with her that I had attempted to tackle this road of coursework with the encouragement of my professors. However, after a while, I felt it was best that I quit at the specialist level.

To my amazement and puzzlement, my new colleague friend began to ask me weekly if I'd resumed my program of study. She didn't accept my many excuses, and she nudged me to reconsider trying again because I had come so far. Magically, luckily, and Godly, a "complete your degree" personal trainer appeared on the scene. This type of "confidence-building" went on for months. January, February, March, April, May—she'd ask lovingly if I'd gone back to graduate school to finish the program of study that I had started. My answer was always a pathetic no. And silently, I thought, "Leave me the hell alone! I'm done!" I am tired!!!

Meanwhile, trouble began to brew at work. I was having a lot of conflict with my new supervisor and new team of teachers. The bottom fell out when my supervisor, out of spite, gave me a poor evaluation. We didn't care for each other, so his way of exerting his power was to give me a terrible evaluation. Keep in mind that I kept all of my accolades in a spiral notebook from 1979 to 2000. Thus, my exemplary work record was documented. To my joy, he lost his battle to discredit me. I am so very grateful that another good colleague, Ms. Connie Finch, had shown me the value of keeping a "career paper trail," just because! A job portfolio, as it was called. It saved my twenty-one-year career.

Reflecting back, I conclude that some of my co-workers were jealous that I was excelling at graduate school work, as well as in my personal life---a new boyfriend had entered my life, a retired Major of the U.S Army with career and money success. So an attempt to take my career and stop me from continuing graduate school was the plot. Sometimes a best friend who knows you the best turns on you. I had a good idea who was going to the administration with details of my life. It failed, like pharaoh's attempts.

In hindsight, things happen for a reason. After that awful year I felt fate was nudging me to say goodbye to my eleven years at Paul West

Middle school that hired me in 1989 restoring my life back to its rightful place; after the demise caused by marrying the wrong guy. I asked to be transferred. Again, a phenomenal sistah friend came to the rescue: Mrs. Jacqueline Hood Williams. With her help, I landed a way less stressful job as a fifth-grade elementary school teacher. Tie it all together—all things work together for good for those who love the Lord!

Well, with a six-month dropout period, a personal doctoral encouragement trainer, and a less stressful teaching position, through no effort of my own, I was set up to be able to resume the Ed. D. program. Unexpected events unfolded without force. They smoothly came together without an ounce of manipulation from me. I was truly OK admitting defeat. Three degrees were quite cool to me. Why bother, I reasoned, with the demands and pressures of a doctoral degree? I had other friends who had dropped out and said to me 'It's just not worth it', how wrong they were.

Well, when the Omnipotent Source has a plan for your life, it will be carried out, like a current in a river that flows without human help. You'll come out amazed and humble at His love, wisdom, and infinite power. Smooth operator God, after a much-needed break of one semester. I faced the professor whose class I abandoned, which was a retake class for failing the statistics section of my Ed. D. comprehensive exam, and proceeded with my atonement steps. I was there to face my defeats- it was far harder to quit than to inch forward- despite my daily fears of "not being good enough." I was plagued with these sensations often. Regardless, I pressed forward. I slowly gained weight because I didn't know how to handle the pressure and fears. I ate way too much! But my food behaviors were much improved!

My Red Sea moment presented itself and it left me without words. While retaking the statistics class my professor gave me weekly makeup assignments to get the incomplete grade removed. I met with him on a weekly basis with the completed assignments. A few weeks into our weekly routine, he "*leans*" into me, and says, "I'm quite pleased with your work and your work ethic. I've got a surprise for you: I have personally selected you as my Ed. D. candidate and I will be your dissertation chairperson."

Next, he said to me, "Do you know how lucky you are to have me as your chairperson? I only take on the best of the best!" I smiled in bewilderment, for I was unable to take it all in, not knowing what to say. Is this real? Oh, my God! Oh my goodness! Right before my eyes, the person who would guide, support and ensure that I complete my dissertation appeared (I went into my mental war room; Jesus, Jesus, Jesus!), for without him as my lighthouse on the shore, guiding me to land from the vast sea, completing this portion of the Ed. D. was of no avail. Dr. Persuad, of Indian descent, was my rock! He was a very talented professor.

Under his wing for the next four years, I researched, I wrote, and I rewrote. Dr. Persuad would, critique, suggest, recommend, and direct. Unable to type, I hand-wrote every single word; my words became sentences, which became paragraphs; and paragraphs became pages, which became chapters. This eventually became a published dissertation, a study. My title: <u>The Inclusion of Character Education and Its Impact on Student Discipline in Selected Elementary Schools.</u> To help with the load, I solicited the help of a statistician, a typist, and an editor. A dissertation is similar to a movie production; it takes many experts, many professionals to mold it into a finished product. There was great joy in knowing I had something to say to the world, and it was supported with evidence far beyond a flimsy opinion.

My natural science ability was the sassy spice sprinkled throughout this educational adventure. Science is the search for answers to the world around us. I had done and completed an exhausting research project of six chapters, to answer a question about a social phenomenon that was on the rise. "Would teaching character education (values and morals) decrease school discipline problems? Whew, sing—"ain't gonna hurt nobody to get on down." At last, I was getting down and knee-deep in this study.

And get down is what I had done for four years, while working full time as a teacher leader of science—teaching students and training teacher candidates. A divorced, single mom of a now teenager and one adult son, had persevered. My plate was full; however, my focus, tenacity and strength came from God and my spiritual family and friends.

I could envision the finish line, the end zone...my Academic Super Bowl...World's Highest Degree, LAWD!!! I fought back the tears; born in the crack, but didn't fall through: speechless...The almost there aroma was buttery sweet, propelling me to push to the final frontier: the doctoral defense—the last major step! The Academic World Olympics was upon me: the pressures, the stress, the fear—but you do it anyway. This is what you've trained for the last seven years. It's too late to turn back now.

All doctoral students fear this moment. Presenting your dissertation to the department (several professors along with your dissertation chairperson), and other doctoral students can produce a paralyzing fear, a panic attack that can destroy all of your hard work. So I took deep breaths, and I reflected on each trial and tribulation. I had invested seven years in this degree: three years of doctoral coursework, a five-hour, two-day comprehensive doctoral exam, I retook one class, due to failing one section on the Ed. D. comprehensive exam, and another mandatory supportive writing class for minor deficiencies in my writing structure. I dropped out, quitting for six months. Then there were the four years of writing scrutiny and tutoring. As I reflected upon each trial and with that in mind, I bit the bullet and pressed on.

My fear shrank and "Let's do this last step" won out. I had to decide either Tragedy or Triumph; a no-brainer. Once again I was at a fork in the road. As it is with life, the next obstacle appeared---now that the decision to move forward was established---my lack of computer skills slapped me in the face. Being overloaded with graduate school and career; I hadn't learned how to do the new PowerPoint slides or how to work the PowerPoint program required by CAU to defend my dissertation.

There are many sacrifices when deciding to get an Ed. D. and this was one of them. I was suspended in time, as far as computers go. I was still using transparencies and an overhead projector in my classroom. Like Rip Van Winkle, I had been asleep not twenty but seven years and if you add my MA degree, I'd been asleep ten years. My professors were impressed by my genuine hard work and continued learning. First impression is everything, so I knew without a doubt that I had to deliver my doctoral defense with PowerPoint slides and use a CD ROM data-storage disk as expected by my esteem professors. But how was I going to pull this off? The outdated transparencies method of presenting material would definite kill any chance of graduating. It was clear I should ask for help. I was surrounded by super-talented teachers. A sistah friend took the pledge! Ms. Vonda Shands.

Need I say it, "The Red Sea" had parted again! I should probably nickname myself, "Moses Jr."...hearty laugh, chuckle, chuckle, chuckle!!!

A teacher friend miraculously chose to transfer to my new school to teach fifth grade the same year I transferred. This was totally unplanned on my part which made it so much more affirming to me that GOD was with me- the King of Kings. We became close friends and I shared with her my liability of not knowing the latest computer programs. And one glorious day, out of the blue, she offered to take an afternoon after work to help me and the two of us put together a first-rate PowerPoint presentation.

To this day, Ms. Shands thinks her role was insignificant, that all of the facts were there in my dissertation, and that she merely typed as I chose the facts to be used. As the Marvin Gaye's lyric sweetly said, "It takes two, baby; it takes two, baby!" Me and you. Without her technological smarts, this last task could have been the straw that broke the camel's back. I was mentally unable to learn another thing at this time. Her non-judgmental help with this computer program was beautiful. This long, draining process had taken its toll on me. I needed a soft place to land. It was her…standing with me that held me together—a warm hug for this weary soul.

She and I have a strong connection, as I am so indebted to her. This was huge for me. Unlike my first family, she was the wind beneath my wings, for I was standing on fumes, fumes of vapor, because there is only so much you can absorb.

I wanted this seven-year roller-coaster circus jump through the fiery ring to be over. I was limping to the end of the ride with mixed emotions—joy, pain, exhaustion, fear, fright, triumph, anger, and the beat goes on, I mean, the list goes on.

The date was set by the department on the special bulletin board in the hall of my building. I walked by that board many a day and saw other doctoral students' announcement of their scheduled defense and sighed, 'would I ever see my name on this board'. Fantasy-real…It said "February 26, at 1:00 p.m., Bonita J. Gay-Senior will defend her dissertation." I walked by the board many times just to convince myself that it was true. I asked a classmate to take a picture of me standing by the board with my fingers pointing to my very own announcement prepared by the department. Woo hoo!

A day or two before the defense, I blocked everything out, and taught myself to work the university's computer and monitor and practiced presenting my dissertation defense of seven years via PowerPoint. Keep in mind that just one day before, I didn't have any experience with the PowerPoint program, university computers, or using disks. I prayed to steady myself. I thought, "Finally, this frightmare will be over tomorrow."

The minutes seemed like hours, and the hours seemed like days. Dear God, please let tomorrow arrive—I am so tired of this project, and it's too late; too late to turn back now, I believe. I believe I'm falling in love, and I believe I'm about to defend my dissertation and finish. I could, on some small level, connect with Jesus's pain of "It is finished" when he was crucified on the cross! Father, the world doesn't know what we go through to finish our doctorates, and that's OK most of the time, because I know you do, dear God. Knowing this was your will for me keeps me humble. My will was to cave in, to quit, and to say, "It's too hard!"

At last, that glorious day arrived, but to my horror and dismay, Atlanta was snowed in. Schools and colleges and universities were closed. I cried out to God, "I can't wait another day! I want to breathe again!"

My wonderful teacher friend, Ms. Shands, had told me about the possibility of inclement weather on my defense day, and I wouldn't hear of it. She'd supportively laughed —my expression was hysterical. Jokingly yet seriously, I retorted, as I often did, "Where is the razor blade? I'm going to cut my wrists!" That was my way of coping with my pain — no intention of carrying it out, because I had a lot of supportive friends from my study groups. It just felt good to say it out loud.

With the choking burden of this dissertation defense around my neck and weighing heavy on my heart, all I could do was pray and repeat fervently, "Jesus, Jesus, Jesus: help me hold it all together." My state of mind mirrored "Enough of this flippin' degree." To fan the flames, my two beloved Cocker Spaniels had run away that week, and keeping it real, y'all, I had no strength or time to go out and look for them. Crap was piling up, as it always did. I did my prayer thing of surrendering—what's gon' be, it's gon' be. I'm powerless but not helpless. I'm only human, don't ask too much of me, too soon.

In the meantime, I just sat and stared out of the window, remembering what my friend who had helped me with the PowerPoint had said the day before: "Bonita, you know it's supposed to snow and ice over tomorrow." I retorted, "No, it just can't." I refused to entertain such a horrific thought.

Beauty is as beauty does! In my solo chamber of fright, my cell phone rang. "Hello," I said. It was my dissertation chairperson, Dr. Persuad. I braced myself for cancellation of my dissertation defense due to the poor weather and driving conditions. Then he said, "We will come today to evaluate your defense and determine if you qualify for the doctor of education degree for May 2004 graduation." I was so happy that my professors showed empathy for me, and came out in such dangerous conditions. That was the culture of Clark Atlanta University. They were there for the students...a university of EXCELLENCE! Wow, I love that school and the whole university!

"Yes, great, I'll be there!" Superman and Batman had nothing on me in that moment. I put on my Wonder Woman gear, swooped up my Dunkin' Donuts, juice and refreshments for the committee, my PowerPoint, and several copies of my six-chapter dissertation, and cautiously drove to Clark Atlanta University.

The professors, visitors, and classmates all arrived, and were seated by 12:50 p.m. I offered them refreshments. One professor smiled and said, "Donuts and snacks won't sway my evaluation one bit!" He chuckled, but I knew he meant it. In other words, "This better be worth my time, my drive in this dangerous, unsafe weather."

Instantly, I thought to myself, "I know this research study inside and out; it has been my constant companion for four years. Do your thang, Bonita! Don't let anything, or anyone frighten you." With that in my mind, I presented my six chapters to the committee, one PowerPoint slide at a time. I did my research on a rising problem in public schools--- The increase of discipline problems and the decrease of respect for Teachers from both students and parents.

From the 1980s to the present, I was in the educational trenches watching the steady decline of morality amongst parents and students. Principals and assistant principals were flooded with disciplinary office referrals from teachers. In order for them to manage these mounting student write ups, the classroom management styles of teachers came into question. This horrendous trend was taking its toll on the once honored career of educating America's youth.

This turn of events in public schools led to my doctoral research. I felt strongly that religion should be restored to the classrooms. Surprisingly, after reading tons of articles on the subject it became crystal clear why our forefathers: James Madison, Thomas Edison, Ben Franklin, Roger Williams and others made the decision to separate church and state (public schools).

These deeply religious men knew firsthand from living in their homeland of England what happens when a government is in charge of choosing one accepted religion for the country. England executed widespread persecution against any person that did not worship with the specified Christian sect. In addition, full citizenship was denied.

With that being said, the first American politicians built a wall of separation between church and state as seen evident by the first Amendment of the U. S. Constitution of 1791 which states, in short, that "all Americans have freedom to practice the religion of their choice, free speech, free press and the freedom to peacefully assemble and announce grievances."

So, how do teachers teach moral reasoning skills and values yet still honor the laws of the land? Scholars such as Kirkpatrick, Schaeffer, Jones, Lickona and others recommend the solid long-term solution of Character Education. Which is the continuous process of aiding young people in establishing good character (morals, virtues), i.e. fairness, honesty, compassion, responsibility, and respect for self and others. Advocates of Character Education argue that teaching these moral traits can decrease violence and juvenile crimes, reduce fights and vandalism, lower suspension rates and increase student achievement. A Dr. King quote sums it up well, "Intelligence plus character – that is the true goal of true education."

I randomly selected nine elementary schools in a large school system that taught Character Education and asked if they'd participate and complete a 74 questions survey developed by my distinguished chairperson, Dr. Persuad and me. The numbers from the surveys were crunched and the data revealed that most definitely the teaching of virtues does in fact decrease student disciplinary problems in public schools.

Next, I answered the professors' questions. It flowed as smooth as ocean waves. They were all very satisfied, and unofficially, they unanimously pronounced me "Dr. Bonita J. Gay-Senior." It was unofficial, as there were more steps for the department to complete as well as verify that I had made the minor corrections they recommended. Nonetheless, my defense was done. This process was so grueling that I didn't have the time to take a graduation picture or receive a yearbook. I regret not having the time to do those two small yet significant things, but it is what it is; a drawback of being a single parent with little or no blood family help.

Two months later, graduation day finally arrived, May 2004. I walked across the stage of Clark Atlanta University in a doctoral cap and gown with the bars on the sleeves and received my doctorate of education. I had friends and family there to share my moment: mom Beulah, my sister Debbie, brother Billie Rank, sons, and so forth. It was my Mary Tyler Moore moment: "You're gonna make it after all."

After receiving my degree on stage, I walked down each step to the floor in utter disbelief. Like the story of *The Velveteen Rabbit*, "It takes a long time to become real, by that time, you have been bruised and scarred without mercy." With thoughts flushing through my head, I removed my graduation cap and tossed it in the air, mimicking Mary Tyler Moore's memorable hat toss humming "You're gonna make it after all!" from the iconic song, "Love Is All Around Us" by Sonny Curtis. This time I sang several verses. "Who can take a nothing day, and suddenly make it all seem worthwhile. You are most likely to succeed, you have the looks and the charm and girl you know that's all you need."

A few months later, I had an epiphany about the awesomeness of The Source of Creation (God) evenly present and omnipotent. As I drove past the university parking lot, reminiscing on my blood, sweat, and tears degree, the revelation of what occurred on May 2004 sent sirens tingling astonishment sparks throughout my mind. I made a startling connection—God had brought all my years of travels together in that one day. I had lived on the same street as Clark Atlanta University as a child. Chestnut Street and James Brawley Dr. are the same road. The name changes when it crosses over a medium-sized intersection. In order words, don't faint, smelling salt please. I obtain my Doctorate of Education on Chestnut Street!!! The awareness of this never crossed my mind until that day after I had graduated. Now, that's 100 as the millennium say.

We are not alone in the universe. That's the mysticism of spirituality. Like the Israelites, I had wandered in circles, in the valley, and darkness for 40 years before entering into the promised land of milk and honey. I made many detours for over forty years, only to arrive at my destination less than a few miles up the street from my childhood 'House of Terror' home. It's indescribable! But GOD!

I was there all the time. Like Dorothy in *The Wizard of Oz*, I had the power to reach my goal but I didn't believe it. I had to follow my yellow-brick road of many twists and turns only to find I could have gone home (Clark Atlanta University) at any time. I was born on the same street that my University is on! I received my degree in the university's stadium also on the same street. If you look close enough, God will show himself in plain sight.

Can you imagine how it feels to witness this chain of events, perfectly lined up. Many years earlier I had been called fat, ugly, black, and bald-headed. I had been abused, neglected, living in poverty; had an alcoholic father and a smart mentally unstable mother. And then to find myself walking across the stage at Clark Atlanta University to receive the highest degree in the world, an Ed. D., or doctor of education...There's no one like God. There's definitely no one like God...Amen!

My Doctoral Research Project

According to my upbringing from home, church and school, I had a deep connection to religion. I was fascinated with this God subject.

Exuberance exploded in my young body as I observed the grown-ups honor this mystical force that appeared to take care of all people and all things simultaneously.

My young insides felt warm and jubilant, with a yearning to know more about this Universal Power that had all the grown-ups in my world in awe. My teachers seemed bigger than life and bowed to him, Mother Beulah revered him as seen clearly through her action of getting all six of us to church many Sundays via bus or taxicab. Neither my mom nor grandma owned a car at that time.

At my Public Elementary School, E.R. Carter, which is now closed morning devotion was the first subject of the day. The lower grades K-4 gathered in the long second level hall. Here we sang songs of praise and worship and recited the Pledge of Allegiance to the flag. This was our daily routine and I looked forward to it. I felt the flow of Agape Love; so different from human Eros Love.

The teachers, Mrs. Lily, Mrs. Quarterman and Mrs. White engaged with us as we gave honor to the Creator. They discussed various related spiritual topics and lead us in song and the spoken word. I saw another side of them that I liked a lot; soft and gentle. These teachers transformed from stern disciplinarians into kind and happy people of faith. I liked what I saw in them....I liked it somewhere deep in my being that I couldn't articulate.

I remember feeling my happiest at these morning activities. The entire lower grade levels became one big unit... a blissful sight for my eyes to see. Ain't no sight like this one to this little girl. It took my breath away. I swelled with curiosity about God and his practices. It was my first experience with Unity in the educational environment – being on one accord with purpose.

Later on in life I came to realize that I really admired togetherness for a common cause of Goodness...of Greatness. In my elementary school, years ago, the common cause was to honor someone bigger than all of us –The Universal Presence!

Many years would pass before I re-activated the memories of those early days of religion and public schools housed under the same roof. By this time I was a public education teacher myself.

I was in the trenches watching the steady decline of morality amongst parents and students. The level of disrespect toward teachers also continued to rise. Principals and assistant principals were overwhelmed with the increasing numbers of office referrals for discipline.

In order to manage the situation teachers were blamed. Our classroom management styles were called into question. The Educational Institution boat was rocking trying to find some level of equilibrium. I'm in the middle, like a deer caught in the headlights. I loved my profession not so much the salary and now this new trend had taken its toll on the once honored career of teaching children to read, write, do math and think…was sinking like the Titanic…unimaginable! I was devastated some days, other days I looked for the success with some students, and some parents. These two extremes were always present.

This turn of events in public schools led me to my doctoral research. I began my doctorate program project of six chapters in 1997 solely because my professors repeatedly encouraged me to pursue the degree. I was still healing from my traumatic childhood life and felt that getting an Ed. D. was beyond my reach. However, with much prayer and shaking in my bones, I took the plunge. I chose the title "Character Education and Student Discipline in Selected Elementary Schools." Many pieces of my life experiences were coming together now, such as loving the learning process and religion which I showed proudly.

I felt strongly that religion should be restored to the public schools; couldn't even fathom why it was outlawed in the first place! Dang it!! Surprisingly, after reading what felt like tons of articles on the subject it began to make sense why the forefathers: James Madison, Thomas Jefferson, Ben Franklin, Roger Williams and others made the debatable decision to separate Church and State.

These deeply religions men made the sacrifice to openly support multi-religions for the sake of our country. They had first-hand experience of what happens when a government is in charge of choosing the one accepted religion for the country. In England, their homeland, the government executed widespread persecution of any person that did not worship the specified Christian sect. In addition, full citizenship was denied. On that note the first American politicians felt it best to build a wall of separation between church and state. Schools are a ward of the State.

All of this is what led to how I landed upon my research topic adventure. I couldn't go through the front door, so I entered from a side door. This way I would not violate the U.S. Constitution Amendment of 1791, in short Americans have the freedom to practice the religion of their choice, along with free speech, free press, free to peacefully assemble and freedom to announce grievances.

Consequently, how do classroom teachers and schools teach moral reasoning skills and values and still honor the laws of our land? Schaeffer, Kirkpatrick, Jones, Lickona and others recommend giving up the band-aid approach and look toward long term solutions such as character education.

The continuous process of aiding young people in establishing good character (morals and virtues), i.e., fairness, honesty, compassion, responsibility, and respect for self and others. Advocates of character education argue that teaching these moral traits can help decrease school violence, juvenile crimes, reduce fights and vandalism, lower suspension rates and increase academic achievement. Thus, my research was about the development of character in pupils.

I wholeheartedly concur with the statement made by Martin Luther King, Jr., in The Reporter, 2000, p.28, where he states "Intelligence plus character --- that is the goal of true education."

I desire to be a *True Educator*, imparting knowledge *and* a sense of what is right and wrong to my students and my two sons at home. William

Kirkpatrick sums the concern up by saying "In addition to the fact that Johnny can't read, we are now faced with the more serious problem that Johnny can't tell right from wrong." (Jones, 1998 p. 15)

I randomly selected nine elementary schools from a large school system. I asked if they would participate in my study via a seventy-four question survey developed by me and my distinguished dissertation chairperson, Dr. Persuad.

These elementary school teachers were teaching Character Education and could give valuable data about the results of teaching youngsters virtues that can last a lifetime. These virtues taught in school lined-up with their Sunday school lessons, no matter their religion or lack of a religious affiliation.

Personally, I am a non-denominational New Thought Unity Christian Truth Student. I am a friend of Hillside International Chapel and Truth Center, under the leadership of Founder Bishop Dr. Barbara Lewis King, in Atlanta, Georgia, since 1984. Many *Spiritual* and *Religious* persons have spoken at my church such as poet and author, the late Dr. Maya Angelou, talk show host Oprah Winfrey, "Fix My Life" host and Coach, Iyanla Vanzant and many more.

After four years of studying and writing… this topic blossomed into a six chapter dissertation now published in the Library of Congress. Its results conclude that the character of a child must be taught by others to produce good citizens in our society and world!

My Two Sons

There was a classic Television Show entitled "*My Three Sons*" starring Fred McMurray and I emulated the TV dad's parenting style of being present and involved with my two sons. Except wouldn't you know it, unexpected tragedy landed in my life. Both of my sons had near death childhood illnesses where hospitalization was their only chance of survival to experience life into adulthood and beyond.

Kornelius, my first son, began to swell around his eyes, ankles and feet. He was a child who was full of energy and his eyes had lost their shimmer. His desire to go outside and play had evaporated completely. When I gave him a meal, he pushed it back at me complaining of being sleepy. Baffled, I called the only mother I knew – mom Beulah. She told me to quickly take him to Grady Memorial Hospital Emergency room in Atlanta. Full of gripping fear, I drove the 20 minutes to the hospital and prayed the whole time.

After an examination, a series of questions and tests, Kornelius was diagnosed with Nephritis Syndrome, a liver disease. My one and only question was can it be treated and if he could be restored to excellent health? After a frightful day of unknowns, the doctors assured me that he could indeed be treated and would fully recuperate as a healthy child.

I gave my consent to proceed with medications and getting a room ready for my son. My Mrs. Fred McMurray came out (from the TV series) when I asked the nurse to give me a sleeping cart so I could stay with him. I was not going to leave his hospital room until he was well. Ms. Bonita and her one son at the time stuck it out! That's right, I was present and involved in my son's life as much as humanly possible based upon my raising. As Dr. Phil says, "Sometimes you gotta rise *above your* raising!"

After a few days in the hospital and much improved, Kornelius was released with a treatment plan: stay away from salt, drink mostly water and continue to take his prescribed medications. I was relentless about giving him water. I would sit out four bottles each day. We would sit together in the living room as I watched him drink every ounce while watching his favorite TV shows: The Incredible Hulk, Dukes of Hazzard, etc.

My second son, Edward H. Senior V got struck with a life threatening illness at age four. Dang! I have the best of luck!! Walk a mile in Bonita's moccasins—whew --- unbelievable! I was bewildered when Edward lost all of his muscle function in his arms. I would lift his arm up and it would fall down, he had no control of his muscles and was nearly paralyzed. He only wanted to sleep, and that was a sure sign he wasn't feeling well. This was one active, playful child just like his brother Kornelius!

I took him to a private doctor who basically didn't know what to do so he sent us home. Glory be to God, when I got home I checked my phone messages and the Doctor had left a panicky message on my phone strongly instructing me to get him to the Scottish Rite Children's Hospital in North Atlanta immediately. By golly, within a few hours, Edward H. Senior V was diagnosed with spinal meningitis and was swiftly admitted to the hospital. The illness was a swelling of the membranes around the spinal cord and brain. I was scared motionless.

It is said 'absence makes the heart grow fonder', well I am going to expand that to the "potential of absence also makes the heart grow fonder." Since both sons experienced life threatening diseases at a young age a bond of deep love was created that connected us like no other force. I would fight a Goliath if it threatened their chance of life and a good upbringing.

Edward stayed in the hospital for weeks making gradual improvements. Again, I requested my sleep cart so I would be there with him. Several days into his stay I was hit with the "you don't have medical insurance" dilemma. I called my new supervisor at the College cafeteria where I was a cook and server and told her my situation. She calmed me down by telling me she would make sure all the documents were dated appropriately and sent in to the insurance company. Further, she apologized for the inconvenience! Woop…woop…God in skin again! This act of kindness saved my child's life. I never again heard about any lack of insurance.

After weeks of treatment, Edward was released without permanent damage to his brain and a zero balance on his hospital bill…incredibly amazing--- a fantastic moment. My God hugs, as I called them kept me inspired and hopeful. Hope is a powerful force. Things seemed to work out for the best if I just kept doing the next right thing; the next healthy thing.

When Kornelius was eight, he won a turkey for Thanksgiving at the Boy's Club he attended. We really needed that bird, money was scarce that year as I had recently separated from Edward H. Senior III. The moving expenses had gotten the best of me. What an awesome son, trying to help me have a Thanksgiving dinner. I was glad he was my son and that he had taken an interest in helping me. This type of support didn't come easy in my first family – it was practically non-existent.

He was also in the elementary school talent show as Michael Jackson and by the end of the contest, he had two girlfriends!! He and I had good times together and I felt wonderful knowing he felt secure enough to get on a stage and perform. I attempted to do this when I was in elementary school and had a full blown panic attack during rehearsal....my group... understandably cut me. I froze from internal criticism that I heard daily in my home. So this was a huge victory for me that at least Kornelius with a "K"...lol...was able to complete his performance as MJ.

After a brief separation, I did agree to re-marry Edward H. Senior III. "I is married now two times". Within a year or so our first child together Edward H. Senior V was born.

Like his brother, he also got to experience typical childhood activities. He was baby Jesus at his daycare center at age one, next he was Master of Ceremony at his daycare Christmas program. All the things I missed as a child because I was emotionally wounded, they were able to experience. I would get parts such as dance in the Christmas play or be an Easter bunny but mother Beulah would storm out of the program criticizing me for not being good enough or having a bigger role. Oh the stench of her disapproval was too much to bear. On the other hand, it gave me sheer joy to give these social opportunities to both of my sons.

I signed up for the Atlanta Big Brother's program to get Kornelius a positive male role model as neither dads where in my children lives. Kornelius was paired up with mentor Attmore. This successful African-American guy volunteered to do service with this program out of the goodness of his heart. As a result, Attmore and Kornelius went on bimonthly outings. This gentleman even bought Kornelius his first car.

Edward H. Senior V and Kornelius D. Ringfield did well in school… *good enough* as one author puts it. Kornelius graduated with a book scholarship, a hard working student certificate/pin and he also received an acceptance certificate to Savannah State University.

They both played sports and won lots of trophies.

Once Kornelius graduated from high school there were a few years of him dabbling into thinking the grass was greener on the other side as mentioned earlier! After that 'Nonsense Chapter', he settled down and did a 180. He married his high school sweetheart in 2000. He and Sonata Lyons Ringfield have two talented young adult children now…Jayvin and Jada. Kornelius also coach a football and basketball until his children grew up. Presently, he and Sonata advanced to owning a lovely home and upscaled cars. He continues to be a "hard working person" just as his high school teachers said he was when they awarded him the "Hard Working Student" award in his senior year. I could not be more proud of him!

Edward H. Senior V, is 10 years younger than his brother Kornelius. Edward has completed college with a B. A. in Sociology and has completed his M. A. in Community Counseling. He has practiced as a licensed therapist and is currently pursuing his real estate license as well. Update, he has passed the real estate test and is a licensed realtor.

Edward is engaged to his long-time girlfriend, now fiancée Ashley Hopkins (wedding in a few months). They have two children Jada and Alana.

My choice to be a *healthy single parent* has paid off. I was motivated to get well for these two individuals…no regrets. I feel victorious seeing each of them excel as excellent ….near perfect human beings. Humans were never meant to be perfect---that idea is so dysfunctional and creates a lot of pain. They are *Good Enough*… what more could a survivor like me ask for? (OMGTY) Oh My God …Thank You!

Here is the icing on the cake! They don't let a day go by without letting me know how proud they are of what I overcame through the years. I humbly thank them and stay centered knowing that God is and was the source that made it all happen. I just answered the call...His Call; we all have that option! Further, He doesn't call the qualified, He qualifies the caller.

A Reflection

I had two so-called pretty boys in my lifetime. They considered themselves so pretty that the woman in the relationship owed them, and therefore, she should provide for them.

Yeah, most people infected with low self-esteem have a certain way of living — I hypnotically went along with unbecoming actions from myself and others. Fast forward... this relationship style left me in a predicament whereby my lease to purchase a new home was denied, my new furniture was repossessed, and my good credit destroyed.

It seems like a movie now. Years later, as the fog clears, I see the unhealthiness of my past. How could a situation of such magnitude escape me? "Duh, Bonita, you are a Cum Laude college graduate with a successful career as a lead teacher." Yet I couldn't handle romantic relationships. For some mysterious reason another force was at work. Rewind—it was coming from my damaged childhood and adolescence; the power of those years is huge and cannot be underestimated.

The other pretty boy made no financial contribution to our relationship. And I can see now that I was under a romantic spell: "I put a spell on you, and now you're mine!" I borrow these lines from the song in the movie *Hocus Pocus*.

This story also briefly includes my five siblings; they didn't make it out, and for that, I am deeply sorry. I somehow have had the luck o' the Irish, born on Saint Patrick's Day, and managed with the help of many others to seal my cracked places. As Iyanla Vanzant would say, "I did my work!" There is no magic pill. Again, I'm sorry; however, sugar-coating doesn't do any of us any good.

A Portrait of Me Now

> *For most of us the struggle was long, painful and lonely to the place where we are now.*
>
> Hazelden

A lot of years have come and gone since my beginning on 280 Chestnut Street. My life has taken many abrupt twists and turns. Each change, no matter how small or large positioned me to a place of healthy functionalism. After graduation from Clark Atlanta University with my Doctorate of Education, an unexpected blessing appeared.

A classmate and colleague, Dr. Y.N. Johnson, decided to celebrate her achievement by going on a seven-day cruise to the West Caribbean. Upon hearing this, I said, "I would love to join you." With a nod of her head, it was a "Yes, I'd like that very much." I felt like the "Grand Invisible Spirit of the Universe" had just personally delivered a reward to me for sticking it out --- seven grueling years of reading, writing, and studying…the rigor of the dissertation process!"

Such an adventure of getting a doctorate degree was nowhere on my radar. However, I'd settled into a daily routine of being open to the flow of unplanned events and believing in the wonder of The Divine Force that allows orderly directions to appear which solves daily living problems.

We packed our bags and off to the seven seas we went. I bathed in the sun, visited various islands, shopped, petted dolphins and turtles. Each moment of my new life was embraced with deep humility and boundless levels of gratitude. My past was gone...I was no longer her, the abused frightened girl on 280 Chestnut Street, she was healed!

The upcoming school year, without my consent, I was told by the principal that I was to teach Language Arts. Heartbreak set in, like never before, I loved being an *Instructor of Science*. It was my joy! Even though, I was under mounting anguish about teaching language arts, I remained obedient and stayed in order and performed my assigned task. However, I prayed, cried, prayed and cried some more; my dream job had been snatched away.

Then one mystical day while working with my students a powerful thought from nowhere burst through to my realm of existence. Everything stood still in quietness even though I was in a classroom full of students. This voice said, sweetly with conviction and clarity, "watch how I work this out"! I looked around to see if my pupils heard the voice too. They had not because they were busy doing their independent practice work. Getting that confirmation that everything was going to work out regardless of how things looked, gave me the gladiator courage to take steps to free myself from this Language Arts teacher career misery.

I resigned at the end of that school year even though corporate headquarters (School District Central Office) said I was under contract and if I broke it there would be dire consequences which included that never working again as a teacher. What the school district failed to comprehend is that I was under God's contract. I knew what He had told me. I knew what I knew!!!

Immediately after I resigned, fear reared its ugly head. I went home, collapsed on the bed and curled up into the fetal position shivering like a leaf. "What in tarnation had I done?" I just walked away from an $85,000.00 a year job and had two mortgages, which I increased to three in 2006! My increased salary was the result of my years of experience and having my doctoral degree.

Nonetheless, I stood on faith. I knew what I heard that glorious day in my classroom. Through a series of unplanned events within a few weeks, I was hired before the interview ended at **Garrett Middle School (GMS)** as a Lead science teacher. This job came with leadership status that neutralized any prior contract with any dang school system. My towering faith paid off! I did the next right thing as much as humanly possible. I did not know what was to come from working at this school. But unimaginable *aligned events astonished my senses. I saw the face of God; everything I heard from the Spirit World that day in my classroom manifested…it came TRUE!*

My life soared to new levels. Everything I learned at this new school would catapult me to new heights for the **next twelve years. I would use my experiences at Garrett Middle School** (as the Holy Spirit Voice Declared in 2005)to land future jobs such as Director of After School Programs (2015)/GMS: Dr. Y. Minor recommended me for that job, Instructional Teacher Coach (2017)/GMS: Dr. Paige recommended me for the Master Teacher Certification called Teacher Support Specialist(TSS), Clinical Supervisor of Student Teachers from universities across the nation in 2017/ GMS(TSS), and an Empowerment Speaker at Women's Church Conferences(GMS, Dr. Minor). God has more than fulfilled his promise that day in 2005 when he said *"you watch how I work this out."* A person or a skill from Garrett Middle School was instrumental in getting me selected out of other applicants for the aforementioned positions and services; it was all connected!

It was confirmed over and over the following years --- new employers (Bosses) would say to me that because I had the Teacher Support Specialist State Certification License received at Garrett Middle School, as well as nine years of experience with American's Choice Classroom Model, I am excited to offer you this position.

How God pieces all of this together is a "supertastic" mystery…the visible results of his magnificence can't be denied!

Of all of the schools I worked with this school showered me with unsolicited awards. I would sit back in amazement. I was awarded, "The Crystal Apple Teacher of Excellence Trophy in 2008 and 2012; the Dr. Croaker Teacher of Excellence plaque in 2013; and nominated for Teacher of the Year in 2013. I didn't win because I didn't get the most teacher votes, but the grapevine said it was close.

Strangely, within no time after my loss, I was recognized nationally by Covington's "Who's Who Among American's Educators." My principal shared this recognition with the faculty and staff via the school-wide public announcement system. I'm scratching my head --- reacting with sheer humble-ness. This Guiding Power knew in 2005 that this would be happening in 2014! His wondrous works!!! As the late Dr. Wayne Dyer put it, "the synchronicity of events is alive —performing right before your eyes...If you look close enough!"

In 2014, I decided to retire and begin a new chapter elsewhere. You can discern when it is time to change your lifestyle. It was extremely clear to me to release my public school profession. Fear and excitement wrapped my soul – yet despite – these irritants, I permanently separated from my job of thirty-four years to face the unknown.

Within the first year of retirement I was selected to be on the cover of "Women of Distinction" magazine's February 2016 issue. Next, I was featured in an online blog "After the Altar Call" and a guest speaker for the "Women of Virtue Conference" in 2017. I can't wait to see what God is going to do next. What an adventure this is, with Him leading the way!

My redemption did not stop there. While on one of my six-month cycles of no dating, and abstinence from romantic relationships, a guy showed unflinching interest in me. Of course, I was severely cautious – no more frogs for me, please, lol! I adopted the Ruth Boas standard of being independent and confident that my guy would find me – so, in the meanwhile, I fulfilled my life with the joy of others – living as a *thriving* single.

Meanwhile, this gentleman was persistent. I finally agreed to give him my digits…lol—young folks! What did I do that for? He called me each morning at 5:00 a.m. before he went to work. Our conversations got better and better. We progressed to the meet and greet stage. Our first date after many telephone conversations was at an Applebee restaurant for a late lunch. One of my standards included lunch only for first dates and in very public places.

OMGoodness! I was quite impressed with this man's *values* and *character*. I liked how he treated me. He told the waitress to, "Give her whatever she wants!" I had never been treated that way before, so my interest peaked. I thought this may have potential. His demeanor was filled with kindness. He showed a genuine interest in me and making me happy.

To not get lost in my emotions…a prior demon of mine…I was mentally checking off this gentleman's qualities from my self- made relationship chart that consisted of a list of traits that I desired in a partner. My last therapist, Dr. Pamela Thompson strongly advised me to do this exercise. She was point on; this list was my safety net. "Wow, he's getting a lot of checks here," I said to myself. Subsequently, I accepted his invitation to his church as our second date, the next day. He leaned in and gave me a sweet RESPECTFUL kiss as we parted.

While attending his church the next day, to my amazement, he really was who he said he was… a Christian guy very involved in his church who just so happens to be a County Commissioner as well; a step before being a mayor! I used to tell my sistah friends I wanted a 'Barack!' They would tease me implying I was not being realistic, nonetheless, I kept the faith because I know and have experienced that all things are possible with God.

While on some of my many six months no dating phases, some of these same friends would put me down and call me …Man*less*. I tell yah, I think I have a glimpse of what Christopher Columbus went through! The world was saying that the earth was flat yet he dared to believe it was round…explorer daredevil. I get that as I do not conform to the 'group-think' crowd as Dr. Wayne Dyer so eloquently stated in one of his books, "I Can See Clearly Now!" Agreeing to think like the crowd does not allow a person to bloom into their unique organic self. I highly encourage others to, " Go ahead…be True to Yourself, be a human daredevil…UBU (you be you), grinning!

After many telephone conversations, lunches and dates we progressed to a serious courtship over the next three years. He is well liked and respected by my family and friends; even mom Beulah likes him whenever we can be in the same room. To my surprise, he called me one day and said, "I am running for Mayor" and voting is taking place August 2016. Beyond belief, and with 70 million tons of gratitude to God, I said to John, I am proud of you!

I recall when we went to my church the minister from the pulpit looked over at us and said, "Women, if you have a man that is Okay with you doing what you want, cherish him." I assumed she had watched us on several occasions and noticed that Mr. John relaxes in his pew and just let me do my thing at church, he patiently waits while I do my volunteer service as a church greeter. It's the little things that are the big things.

Divine force has healed every area of my life-injured by child abuse and neglect-through church, twelve steps spiritual growth groups and therapy. This powerful combination over time expelled each human weakness. His word is truth as seen in this verse, Luke 13:11 : "And Behold, there was a woman which had a spirit of infirmity and was bowed together, and could in no wise lift herself up, he called her to him and said unto her, 'Woman thou art free from thine infirmity. And he laid his hands on her and immediately she was made straight, and glorified God!" For too many years my ill treatment, disorders, weaknesses, setbacks and disappointments defined me; but no more!"

I honored what the Creator put in me. I also share the details of my life to glorify God. He is no respecter of person, what He did for me He can do for you (Romans 2:11). God does not show favoritism His pure love, gave me the most unimaginable miracle…a resurrected life full of love, forgiveness and redemption!

And so it is……….Amen!

EPILOGUE

WHERE ARE THEY TODAY?

ALL THE PEOPLE AND EXPERIENCES in my life have led me to where I am Today. The lessons were hard but they were learned. I now know that it is possible to love and dislike people at the same time. I know that when a lesson needs to be learned a "teacher or guide" will appear. It is not possible to change others rather you have to change yourself and then your perspective of yourself and others will change without effort!

Mom Beulah: After retiring from her Hair Stylist Salon business, she opened a Room for Rent Company. The venture dried up due to the 2008 housing market crash and the death of her number one helper; her son Kenneth Lee. She eventually returned to her first purchased house. Her health is good at 85 and she is quite active and independent. Mom Beulah never sought mental health support and as a result continues to alienate family members, neighbors and friends. She and I are estranged and barely interact. We are working towards an improved relationship. Sister Baby Debbie has not been seen or heard from since 2007; ten years ago. Brothers Randy and Billie Rank have limited visits with her to avoid the sure to come mental and emotional stabs. I love her from a distance and pray for her, my siblings and myself daily. Each of us is doing the best we can at the moment.

Father Willie Frank Gay: My Dad Willie Frank Gay died in 1972 from a gunshot wound over a street gambling debt. He was absent from my life by the age of four.

Grandmother Mary: Died in 1977 from a stroke. She and her sister Cora were living in the Eagan Home projects where my journey began.

Brother Danny Gay: Eldest brother Danny died in 2015 from complications of his mental condition – Schizophrenia/Paranoia. The voices in his head told him not to take his medications for his high blood pressure. After several strokes Dementia set in. He eventually got mental health support in his late fifties but it was more so to get the disability check as he relapsed often because he would not take his medications. He has one daughter who continues the family cycle of estrangement. Grenda Gay does not communicate with the family and had a turbulent relationship with her Dad –Danny Gay. She has three sons that do not know their Grandmother (Mom Beulah) for the same reasons; her erratic and harmful behaviors.

Brother Kenneth L. Gay: In 1999, at the age of 47, he died due to suicide by police. His mental illness of Schizophrenia (Delusions) was diagnosed by a home visit mental health provider that I initiated, seized his body. He was exhausted, depressed and ready to rid himself of what he said was "an awful existence." He was living with Mother Beulah.

Brother Billie Rank Gay: Became a successful entrepreneur in music, nightclub ownership, building and renovating houses but dare not to help his first family with any of his skills. Presently, his fourth marriage has ended. He has three adult children (Tameka Gay, Kenyanna Gay and Kareem Gay) and six grandchildren. He remains shut off and hostile towards me and other family members. He doesn't talk to us and acts like we are invisible. Also, he openly puts down my many accomplishments and does the same thing to Brother Randy. You can feel his hate/envy for his family of origin fifty miles away! I handle him with a long handle spoon. I do know we both had a terrible upbringing which impacted us negatively.

While I do understand our horror of living on 280 Chestnut with Mom Beulah, he has been the most arrogant and condescending of all of my family of origin – and wouldn't you know it; he is mom Beulah's favorite son! Nonetheless, I wish him the best as each person handles their childhood abuse differently…similar to grief. Once size does not fit all.

Brother Randy Gay: Brother Randy work life is good. He is a security guard and has a small business doing lawn care. He purchased a home many years ago and still lives there! Throughout his life he has made some poor choices with relationships that didn't turn out so well…but haven't we all?! However, he continues to try to improve himself. As with Brother Billie Rank, he has married several times; he is now in his third marriage with one son named Adul from a previous marriage.

He and I are estranged because I became extremely upset when he didn't attend our late brother Danny's funeral. I haven't been able to get past that; nor did Brother Billie Rank attend either. I do get that Brother Danny could be verbally and physically aggressive at times; but he had good days with them too! I expected them to show up to say a final "Goodbye" to the oldest brother who was left home many days to raise us. As Iyanla Vanzant said in one of her episodes *Fix My Life*, "there is a ranking order amongst brothers and sisters and special respect should be shown to the oldest." To disrespect him like that left a sour taste in my soul. I accepted then and there that those two were unconscious on so many levels that it is healthier for me to surround myself with my family of love(spiritual groups, etc.) and release this family of blood because that is all we share is DNA and blood!

Sister Debbie Gay: Sister Debbie has not been heard from since Mom Beulah threatened to shoot her in 2007 over some trivial disagreement when she was visiting her from Boise, Idaho. Debbie was also diagnosed with Schizophrenia, like my brothers Danny and Kenneth shortly after she completed college. Once the total advanced to three with this disorder; a light bulb went on! To be sure I researched and had discussions with health professionals; we were able to conclude that Mom Beulah is a functional schizophrenic and my siblings inherited it from her. This condition comes in many ranges; mild to chronic.

Suddenly, everything made sense; this is why growing up with her was so damn horrific! Finally, I could breathe out a sigh of relief! I was 52, half a century had gone by before I had an answer to my long suffering saga in my original household. Now I knew the "Why" of EVERYTHING! Immense relief and exuberance filled my insides!

X- Husband Edward H. Senior III: Once we permanently separated in 1988, we stopped communicating. What I did learn however, is that he married many times after me. I was marriage number three. He continued to seek easy money through real-estate transactions which eventually landed him in prison for fraudulent activities; he served his time and was released. He refused to be a Dad to his two children; Trisi Senior and Edward H. Senior V. He abandoned both of them, never paid child support for either of them. He presently resides in Florida.

ACKNOWLEDGEMENTS

To thank all the people who helped me write this book would be like trying to count every star in the nighttime sky! Impossible! Apologies in advance; fault it to my head not my heart. Ultimately though, a number of individuals must be thanked; my friend, author, journalist and final editor, Jacqueline Holness- Meredith, who encouraged me to turn my eager volunteer work of mentoring women into a memoir which candidly discussed my missteps and life's lessons. I was hesitant to follow-through because my way of living was my 'normal;' didn't see anything different about it. She then increased her stir of the idea by giving me a copy of a book entitled, "A Piece of Cake" by Cupcake Brown. After reading this book I no longer felt isolated. I was liberated; set free from indecisiveness! Another thanks goes to Christi, Malika, and Melissa for being brave enough to turn over 400 handwritten pages into type print.

In addition, I am extremely thankful for my editing team: Cynthia of Write One, Create Space and Alberta for your honest feedback soaked in loving kindness of my semi-finished book. Further, I'd like to thank Marie Kane who led me to some much needed and invaluable resources whenever I hit a brick wall; ready to sink. Friendships of such magnitude are uncommon but oh so refreshing. You were a guide post in my uninvited wasteland.

A salute of gratefulness to all the institutions and people who supported me and informed me with healthy living knowledge: Hillside International Truth Center, where Bishop Dr. Barbara L. King taught me a brand new path to follow; Clark Atlanta University, Morris Brown College, West Georgia University and Georgia State University for embracing me 'as is' then refining and developing me into a person of academic excellence, character and self-love. Smooches!

To the friends that I'm so fortunate to know that stand with me: Dr. Yolanda R. Johnson, who I mirror more and more, so full of God's love for humanity, a human example of selflessness; Dr. Yolanda Minor, my sister from another mother, always ready to help move the world towards goodness; Sandra Nobles whose giving spirit introduced me to a 'Women's Group' named ' Women Aspiring Together To Succeed' (WATTS) that resurrected my exhausted writing bones back to life... the final onward push to take this book to and across the finish line. The power of like-minded people is phenomenal.

Wholehearted kudos to my sons Kornelius D. Ringfield and Edward H. Senior V for showing up on the planet to give me a reason to overcome my childhood terrors. Your presence put the ball in my court which unequivocally led me to the decision to *intentionally* seek personal growth processes in any reasonable form. As the late Dr. Wayne Dyer stated, "there is massive power in *intentions*!" Because of you dearest sons, I refused to waiver or give up before the miracle happened. And it did happen. Today, years later, I marvel at the lives you two have constructed which includes daughters-in-laws Sonata L. Ringfield and Ashley N. Hopkins Senior, my Grandkids: Jayvin, Jada 1, Jada 2 and Alana.

Equally important, a big shout out to the guy I share my life with, John A. Harris. I enjoy our serious courtship and the manner in which you pursued me...clean and healthy. I am grateful to have such a supportive companion and a safe place to fall when life's tidal waves appear as they sometimes do.

Last but by no way least, I wish to lift up high to the hills the name of God, The Source of Creation, as I understand him to where it rightfully belongs. Too many times unexpected events lined up with no effort of my own that propelled this project forward. Even I couldn't stand in the way of its completion and believe me sometimes I tried. My most memorable situation was when I put my finished written draft under my bed thinking I don't want to do this anymore. I quit!!! Within a short while, a series of unusual events led me to a women's church retreat (it hasn't happened since).

As I sat in a class with a new author whose name was Bonita too as the leader, I was flooded with a *Knowing* that said I would win one of her books with my raffle ticket and that this would be my message from God to get that book from under the bed and complete it.

The rest is history, sure enough my raffle ticket was called (even the workshop leader) was surprised because I was the fourth ticket and she hadn't planned to call but three); so I won her autographed book, entitled, His Daughters (so appropriate).

I turned out that entire class as I couldn't contain myself. I wept the ugly cry! I had a Shout Praise! On the spot I re-surrendered by saying, "Ok Father, thy will not mine be done." I resumed the book project and brought it to completion. By being obedient to the Supreme Creator, a running thesis in my life, I can truthfully say, "You can *Master* your life!" Go Beyond Survive… THRIVE!!!

Made in the USA
Columbia, SC
09 September 2018